Liverpool Park Estates

LIVERPOOL HISTORICAL STUDIES
published for the
School of History, University of Liverpool

1.   Patrick J. N. Tuck, *French Catholic Missionaries and the Politics Of Imperialism in Vietnam, 1857–1914: A Documentary Survey*, 1987, 352pp. **(Out of print)**
2.   Michael de Cossart, *Ida Rubinstein (1885–1960): A Theatrical Life*, 1987, 244pp.
3.   P. E. H. Hair, ed., *Coals on Rails, Or the Reason of My Wrighting: The Autobiography of Anthony Errington, a Tyneside colliery waggon and waggonway wright, ftom his birth in 1778 to around 1825*, 1988, 288pp.
4.   Peter Rowlands, *Oliver Lodge and the Liverpool Physical Society*, 1990, 336pp.
5.   P. E. H. Hair, ed., *To Defend Your Empire the Faith: Advice on a Global Strategy Offered c.1590 to Philip, King of Spain and Portugal, by Manoel de Andrada Castel Blanco*, 1990, 304pp.
6.   Christine Hillam, *Brass Plate and Brazen Impudence: Dental Practice in the Provinces 1755–1855*, 1991, 352pp.
7.   John Shepherd, *The Crimean Doctors: A History of the British Medical Services in the Crimean War*, 1991, 2 vols, 704pp.
8.   John Belchem, ed., *Popular Politics, Riot and Labour: Essays in Liverpool History 1790–1940*, 1992, 272pp.
9.   Duncan Crewe, *Yellow Jack and the Worm: British Naval Administration in the West Indies, 1739–1748*, 1993, 352pp.
10. Stephen J. Braidwood, *Black Poor and White Philanthropists: London's Blacks and the Foundation of the Sierra Leone Settlement 1786–1791*, 1994, 336pp.
11. David Dutton, *'His Majesty's Loyal Opposition': The Unionist Party in Opposition 1905–1915*, 1992, 336pp.
12. Cecil H. Clough and P. E. H. Hair, eds., *The European Outthrust and Encounter: The First Phase c.1400–1700: Essays in Tribute to David Beers Quinn on his 85th Birthday* 1994, 380pp.
13. David Dutton, ed., *Statecraft and Diplomacy in the Twentieth Century: Essays Presented to P. M. H. Bell*, 1995, 192pp.
14. Roger Swift, ed., *Victorian Chester: Essays in Social History 1830–1900*, 1996, 263pp.
15. P. E. H. Hair, ed., *Arts • Letters • Society: A Miscellany Commemorating the Centenary of the Faculty of Arts at the University of Liverpool*, 1996, 272pp.
16. Susan George, *Liverpool Park Estates: Their Legal Basis, Creation and Early Management*, 2000, 192pp.
17. Alex Bruce, *The Cathedral 'Open and Free': Dean Bennett of Chester*, 2000, 240pp.

Liverpool Park Estates

Their Legal Basis, Creation and Early Management

SUSAN GEORGE

Published for the School of History,
University of Liverpool

LIVERPOOL UNIVERSITY PRESS
2000

Liverpool Historical Studies, no. 16
General Editors: C. H. Clough and P. E. H. Hair

First published 2000 by
Liverpool University Press
4 Cambridge Street, Liverpool, L69 7ZU

British Library Cataloguing in Publication Data
A British Library CIP record is available
ISBN 0–85323–409–4

Printed and bound in the European Union by
The Alden Press in the City of Oxford

CONTENTS

List of Illustrations   vi
Acknowledgements   vii
Map and Plans   ix
Photographs   xii

Introduction   1
Park Estates
1. Villa and Park Estates: the social background   5
Landscape and villa 5; Parks 7
2. Leasehold Development   11
Freehold v. leasehold II; Liverpool leaseholds 13; Defects of
the leasehold system 16; Restrictions on freehold 18
3. The History of Restrictive Covenants   27
Rights and restrictions 28; Covenants recognized and
defined 32; Applications of covenant to building schemes 42
4. Covenant-based Building Schemes   47
Statutory building schemes 47; Building schemes by mutual covenant 50;
Enforceability of mutual covenants 53; Building schemes by intention 55;
The judiciary and building schemes 56

Liverpool Estates
5. Liverpool Park Estates: (1) Fulwood Park   67
The Seftons and residential development 65; The suburbanization
of Liverpool 67; A prefatory venture: Princes Park 71;
Fulwood Park established 71; Fulwood Park in operation 74
6. Liverpool Park Estates: (2) Grassendale Park   87
Grassendale Park 89
7. Liverpool Park Estates: (3) Cressington Park   99
Promotion and foundation of the scheme 99; Site preparation
and building works 107; Disputes and development 113;
Forward to the present day 120
Past and Future   127

Appendix: Legal documents   131
Index   157

List of Illustrations

1. Map showing the locations in Liverpool of Fulwood, Grassendale and Cressington Parks

2. Plan of Fulwood Park

3. Plan of Grassendale and Cressington Parks

4. Early twentieth-century postcard view of Fulwood Park Lodge and gates

5. Modern view of Fulwood Park Lodge and gate pillars

6. Early twentieth-century postcard view inside Fulwood Park

7. Modern view of Number 9, Fulwood Park

8. Modern view of Grassendale Park Lodge and gate pillars

9. Early twentieth-century postcard view of the Promenade, Grassendale Park

10. Early twentieth-century postcard view of Cressington Park Lodge and gates, with St Mary's Church

11. Modern view of Cressington Park Lodge

12. Modern view of The Esplanade, Cressington Park, looking towards Garston and its docks

13. Modern view of 'Binbrook', The Esplanade, Cressington Park

Photographs 5, 7, 8, 11, 12 and 13 are by William George

Acknowledgements

This book has its origins in a dissertation which was submitted for the award of an M. Phil. degree of the Council for National Academic Awards, the now defunct body which oversaw Polytechnic degree courses in the 1980s. My then Head of Department, Bernard Jackson, now Professor in the Law Faculty of the University of Liverpool, forcefully persuaded me of the wisdom of undertaking research. The subject was suggested by Mr Joseph Turner, head of one of the sets of Chancery chambers in Liverpool and formerly Professor of Real Property at the universities of both Liverpool and Manchester. He had been concerned over many years in legal questions concerning the local park estates but had never had time to investigate their origins. Sadly, he died before there was a complete draft of the original work but not before I had had the benefit of his wide learning and enthusiasm. After his death, Professor A.H. Hudson of the University of Liverpool kindly agreed to supervise the final stages, together with Professor Penelope Pearce of the then Liverpool Polytechnic who replaced Professor Jackson as Head of the School of Law, Social Work and Social Policy.

I am very grateful to the Trustees of the Parks for their kind permission to use their deeds and other documents without which the study could not have been undertaken, and also their respective solicitors, whose time and facilities were made available to me, as were those of Mrs T.A. Daley, who was then the custodian of the trunk of documents relating to Cressington Park. Messrs Ingledew, Botterell, Roche and Pybus of Newcastle upon Tyne, and also John Mowlem Homes Limited, kindly supplied on request additional information which allowed consideration of the wider significance of such schemes, past and present. Many other people made contributions and I am grateful to all of them. I particularly thank Linda Kerrigan, who typed most of this material twice.

As regards the present volume, I am indebted to the History Department, University of Liverpool, for including this study in its monograph series, to the series editors for advice and criticism, and especially to Professor P.E.H. Hair for his guidance in turning a legal dissertation into a more reader-friendly book.

S.G.

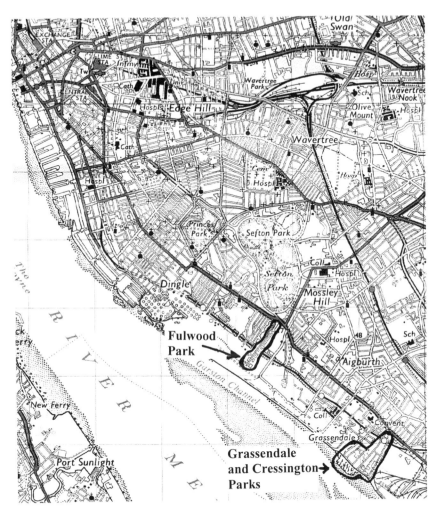

Map showing the locations in Liverpool of Fulwood, Grassendale and Cressington Parks. Reproduced from the Ordnance Survey mapping on behalf of The Controller of Her Majesty's Stationery Office © Crown Copyright. MC 100032438

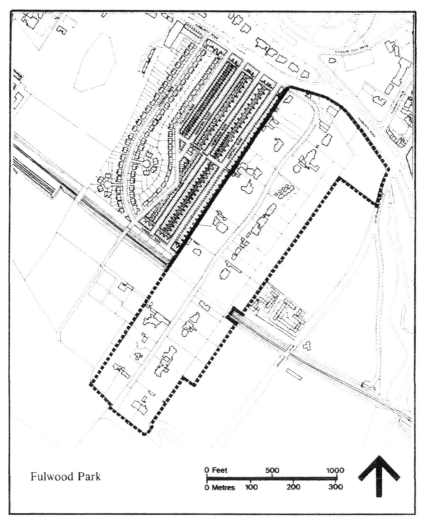

Fulwood Park

Plan of Fulwood Park, taken with with the kind permission of Liverpool City Council from the Fulwood Park Conservation Area leaflet. Reproduced from the Ordnance Survey mapping on behalf of The Controller of Her Majesty's Stationery Office © Crown Copyright. MC 100032438

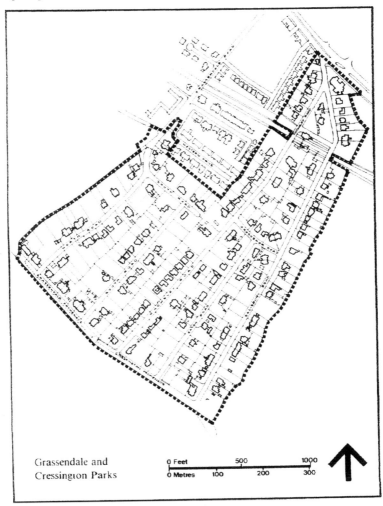

Grassendale and
Cressington Parks

Plan of Grassendale and Cressington Parks, taken with with the kind
permission of Liverpool City Council from the Grassendale and Cressington
Parks Conservation Area leaflet. Reproduced from the Ordnance Survey
mapping on behalf of The Controller of Her Majesty's Stationery Office ©
Crown Copyright. MC 100032438

Early twentieth-century postcard view of Fulwood Park Lodge and gates

Modern view of Fulwood Park lodge and gate pillars

Early twentieth-century postcard view inside Fulwood Park

Modern view of Number 9, Fulwood Park

Modern view of Grassendale Park Lodge and gate pillars

Early twentieth-century postcard view of the Promenade, Grassendale Park

Early twentieth-century postcard view of Cressington Park Lodge and gates, with St Mary's Church

Modern view of Cressington Park Lodge

Modern view of The Esplanade, Cressington Park, looking towards Garston and its docks

Modern view of 'Binbrook', The Esplanade, Cressington Park

Introduction

A recurring urge of human nature is the desire to have a stake in society and roots in a particular place, which in many cultures is manifested in a yearning to own immoveable property, land or a house, or both. In societies that are largely agriculture-based the rationale of owning land is obvious: it represents wealth and power. But the attachment to ownership of land, however limited the area, has continued in the public mind of industrialized societies throughout their urbanization and the declining role of their agriculture. In 1980s Britain the concept of a 'property-owning democracy' was found to be vote-winning.

Legally, what such 'ownership' of land amounts to is a 'bundle of rights', legal rights which have been created by case law over the last nine hundred years and latterly by statute. The land law of England (but not Scotland), as it is today, takes as its starting point the Norman Conquest which superimposed a feudal system on an Anglo-Saxon base. The Crown, in the person of William I, declared that it owned all the land in England and that subjects of the Crown could only have interests in land for a certain length of time. These concepts were gradually refined and defined by the common law, and then codified in 1925, so that we now acknowledge two basic units of landowning time, the longer time-unit being the freehold interest, which is virtually equivalent to ownership for ever, and the shorter being the leasehold interest, which lasts as long as has been agreed between the landlord and the tenant. The freehold of most of the land in England, as in other European societies, was in past time vested in members of the aristocracy, who for long derived most of their income from letting agricultural land to tenant farmers, while retaining the social and political power which came to them from ownership of large estates. But with the advance of industrialization and urbanization, roughly from the first quarter of the eighteenth century, other income-earning uses for land became more and more available, notably that of providing land for urban residential development.

The nineteenth century saw the growth of 'leafy suburbs', areas to which the middle classes could escape from the congestion and what they now saw as the traditional squalor of inner towns and cities. There they could raise their family in a house that was either their own, or, if they rented it, still seemed so to their neighbours. While the history of the rapid increase of British nineteenth-century population has been studied both in general and in particular aspects for many decades, it is only in recent years that urban history has become a distinct area of study, with the result that the legal aspect of urban residential growth has as yet received little attention. Where detailed studies of housing development have been undertaken, the concentration has been either on inner-city, working-class housing built for renting, or on architecturally-interesting middle-class suburbs, such as The Park Estate at Nottingham, a leasehold development.

The investigation of housing development has been inhibited and hampered, particularly in its legal aspect, by the paucity of public records. Where sale of a freehold has taken place it is generally difficult to trace a continuous history because the essence of a freehold transaction is that the deeds are private documents, of concern only to the freeholder – unless a boundary or other dispute brings the transaction before the courts and hence into the public domain. In 1925, when the registration of title to land was introduced nationally, the House of Lords (chiefly responsible for the legislation) did not care to jeopardise the reform process by pressing for the Register to be open to public inspection. This right of inspection was only made law in the Land Registration Act of 1990. Most unfortunately and ironically, when the Land Registry recently moved over to computerisation, the contents of the land certificate publicly available were significantly abbreviated (and much of the old card index system was then destroyed), so that only current ownership appears on the Register. The history of a piece of land is therefore in general still not traceable without access to the deeds in the possession of the householder, his lawyer, or the mortgagee; hence research into a series of pieces of land now individually owned is not practical.

There are, however, chinks of light in the obscurity. Because of the long-term interest of the landlord and the defined area of the relevant land, records are more easily available in the case of leasehold estates, or at least those where the researcher has access to a unified body of material held by the landlord or by a local Record Office. Cannadine's major study of the Calthorpe estate at Edgbaston in Birmingham was possible because of the completeness of the archives of the Calthorpe Estate Office. Again, where there has been a unified residential development by way of a building scheme and where the scheme is still in operation, the original overall deeds will still be available for inspection (if this is permitted), and records of a management committee, whether still in private hands or deposited at a Record Office, may be opened to the researcher. Furthermore, if litigation of any significance has occurred, a report of the case will be available in any law library. The reference in the present study to the history of Cressington Park Estate at Liverpool has been made possible because the early records are still in the hands of the management committee — although regrettably those between 1869 and recent times have been lost — and because the committee kindly permitted their inspection. There are unlikely to be many other instances across England where the student of socio-legal institutions can find adequate recording of earlier amenity-led estate development, and this in part explains why the present study concentrates on Liverpool for its examples.

PARK ESTATES

1: Villa and Park Estate: the social background

The population of Britain, which most probably experienced no more than a five-fold increase in the thousand years before the mid-eighteenth century, certainly experienced a five-fold increase in the next one hundred and fifty years. This accelerated growth of population, particularly strong in the nineteenth century, added sprawling urban centres to the only one that had existed previously, London. The mass of British population moved from countryside living to town and city living; and great efforts therefore had to be made to provide urban housing. A struggle to combine sufficient housing with decent neighbourhood amenities resulted in a number of experiments in formal residential planning. Such schemes depended on and also generated developments in land law.

This study deals in the first instance with the legal context of amenity-led residential planning: more specifically, a century and a half of the operation of the law regarding restrictive covenants in freehold and leasehold contexts. The process is then illustrated with reference to one relevant example of residential planning, the 'park estates' of Liverpool. Before discussing the legal developments, it is necessary to explain, briefly, how park estates came about. An alternative name for 'park estates' might be 'villa parks'.

Landscape and villa

In the past, agriculture was the commonest use for land. The use of land for pleasure was at one time uncommon and largely confined to the great landholders, the formal terraces and gardens of their country residences being surrounded by vast parks for hunting. Nevertheless, from medieval times richer townspeople occasionally cultivated 'pleasure gardens', and from the sixteenth century gardening manuals appeared which emphasized rewards in gardening other than the merely economic and practical. The cult of the garden as a refreshment from the woes of living found expression in 1597 when Francis Bacon proclaimed that –

> God Almightie first Planted a Garden. And indeed, it is the Purest
> of Humane pleasures. It is the Greatest Refreshment to the Spirits
> of Man; Without which, Buildings and Pallaces are but Grosse
> Handy-works … .

Meanwhile a wider aesthetic appreciation of the countryside was developing. The post-medieval expansion of the land market, in part due to the 'privatising' of monastic estates, enabled a merchant class to infiltrate the countryside and increase the number of rich landowners. Lacking the feudal militarism of the earlier aristocracy, they encouraged the whole landowning class to pursue a lively interest in 'improving' their residences and parks. One manifestation of this was the cult of landscape.[1] Organized open spaces around mansions, following various fashions of design, were the hallmark of two famous and influential landscape planners, 'Capability' Brown (1715-1783) and Humphrey Repton (1752-1818). In the latter's 1806 work, *An inquiry into the changes of taste in landscape gardening*, an attempt was made to set out principles for improving the natural landscape of a park. One principle, significant for the future, was that of 'appropriation' – 'that command over the landscape visible from the windows, which denotes it to be private property belonging to the place'. The twin cults, of urban garden and country landscape, came together in the nineteenth century concept of the 'park', not only the municipally planned and formally laid-out urban park for public use – of which the earliest was that at Birkenhead, opened in the 1840s – but also the private residential park.

While it was general that those with sufficient wealth to own country houses also kept town houses, a growing 'upper middle class', unable to afford two establishments, instead raised the standard of urban residence, at least for themselves. Demand for building land in growing cities led to the expansion of the suburbs, with an increasing number of houses being built on smaller and smaller plots of land. As the waves of building spread outwards from the town centres, so the wealthy moved even further away themselves, leaving their old town houses to be demolished and new ones built at much higher densities. Mansions gave way to 'villas', private parks gave way to mere gardens. In 1822, John Claudius Loudon, a landscape gardener and horticultural writer, published his *Encyclopaedia of gardening*, and this discussed gardening on many different scales. Loudon categorized the various types of relevant housing, in a manner which charted the gradations of social scale quite precisely. Much of his detailed description of the various types of villa applied to London at that date, but within a few years, villas of similar type were appearing all over the land.

.

Villas, described as being the class of housing below 'mansions', were found in both country and town. Loudon's comment on the country villa was significant.

Moderate extent and the proximity to other villas, constitute the characteristics of this class of residence; but though adjoining lands are not necessary to the character they do not, where they exist, change it, unless their extent be very considerable. Two villas joined together often mutually aid each other in effect, especially as to water and trees.

Similarly Loudon stressed that the necessary appropinquity of town villas could have its disadvantage reduced by common action. 'Where two or more such villas can be formed adjoining each other, the happiest effects may be produced if their owners act in concert at their first planting; and a sort of community of scenery may be enjoyed, without lessening individual privacy and comfort.'[2] Thus, 'appropriation' of landscape could be obtained even in this modest context, the argument being that the view from each villa would take in the grounds of the other and so increase the amenity of both. Here were the seeds of amenity-led residential estates.

Parks

As London grew, the royal hunting parks which had originally surrounded the capital and were often linked to a royal palace, were progressively bounded by urban buildings, nullifying their private use. Hyde Park was opened to the public in the 1630s and Charles II formed St. James's Park and Green Park. A re-shaping of St. James's Park was included in the formation of Regent's Park, designed by John Nash between 1811 and 1826. But this park was of a different nature from the earlier ones since the scheme included the building of half a dozen villas around the perimeter, the economic basis of the project being that the return on the houses would pay for the whole development.[3]. Nash employed the principle of appropriation in developing the park. The villas were surrounded by trees and shrubs in such a way that each villa was invisible from any other, and every villa had an aspect that gave the impression that the whole park formed part of its grounds. Although it was planned that the public should have access to the centre portion of the park, the villas were protected by private gardens leased to the occupants. Furthermore, while the roads through the park were soon opened for access by carriages or those riding on horseback, only in 1841 did the non-private part become accessible to the public at large.

The Regent's Park development was copied elsewhere. Thus, a similar scheme, where housing around the perimeter was expected to pay for the landscaping and laying out of walks for the enjoyment of the surrounding residents, was opened in Liverpool in 1842. Prince's [usually Princes] Park was laid out on 44 acres of land bought for £50,000, to a design by Joseph Paxton and E. Milner. Paxton went on to design Birkenhead Park (1847), the municipal park noted above, and, in London, Crystal Palace, both on its original site (1851) and on its replacement site (1854), the latter being surrounded by a speculative housing development, Crystal Palace Park.

Those eager to move out of congested urban centres into suburban villas expected to enjoy more favourable amenities.[4] In the early and mid nineteenth century such amenities and their planning were unlikely to be provided to any significant extent by municipalities. The organization of villa developments instead involved speculative builders, landowners who either let on building leases or sold the freehold, and even associations of future residents, all of whom had an active concern about, and often a financial stake in, preserving and creating amenities for the new houses. These amenities ranged from the preservation of trees and other admired landscape features to the building of drains and roads – perhaps even to the selection of suitable tenants. Concern about amenities was not least among the designers and residents of villa parks. As a result, from at least the 1830s, all over Britain involved parties were using a variety of legal devices to create and protect for suburban villa dwellers what the dwellers themselves considered a pleasant environment. Preservation of amenity often depended on covenants, that is, contractually binding agreements concerning the use and future development of the land let and the land surrounding it.

For reasons to be discussed later, the new housing was often leasehold and the villa parks, hereafter termed park estates, were no exception. As Wilkie Collins wrote in 1861 –

> Alexander's armies were great makers of conquests; but the modern guerilla regiments of the hod, the trowel and the brick kiln are the greatest conquerors of all; for they hold longest the soil

that they have once possessed ... with the conqueror's device
inscribed on it – This ground to be let on building leases.[5]
Chapter 2 of this study discusses the law of leasehold, how it came into
being, how it stood when the park estates were formed, and how it has
developed since. Chapter 3 discusses the essential legal feature of park
estates, the restrictive covenant, with its history to date. Chapter 4 details the
operation of covenants in relation to estates and residences, in general.
Finally, Chapters 5-7 focus on three park estates at Liverpool, dealing
particularly with their early history in its legal and management aspects.

NOTES TO CHAPTER 1

1.   Literature had discovered landscape earlier: see Kenneth Clarke, *Landscape into art* (London, 1949). Milton, in *Paradise Lost*, describes Eden's hills, rivers, trees and streams in terms which might have inspired the landscape gardeners of the century to come:

A happy rural seat of various view: / Groves whose rich trees wept odorous gums and balm, / Others whose fruit burnish'd with golden rind / Hung amiable, Hesperian fables true, / If true, here only, and of delicious taste. / Betwixt them lawns, or level downs, and flocks / Grazing the tender herb, were interposed, / Or palmy hillock, or the flow'ry lap / Of some irriguous valley spread her store, / Flow'rs of all hue, and without thorn the rose.

2.   J.C. Loudon, *Encyclopaedia of Gardening* (London, 1822), 1: 1024-5.

3.   As with many of the speculative building schemes, money from ground rents did not match the estimates. The Commissioners of Woods and Forests (precursors of the Commissioners of Crown Estates) took the matter up with Nash who recommended that they 'restrain their anxiety for immediate revenue, to give the opportunity of selecting a higher class of tenants, remembering, that as the Park increases in beauty it will increase in value, and that the first occupiers will stamp the character of the neighbourhood'.

4.   The term 'villa' was inevitably degraded and eventually applied, at least by its residents, to any self-contained suburban property with a garden. Mr Pooter no doubt considered 'The Laurels', Brickfield Terrace, Holloway ('a nice six-roomed residence, not counting basement, with front and back garden') a villa. But the villas here discussed were of superior standing. Note, however, that as a reward for virtue, and to his great satisfaction, Mr Pooter was presented by his grateful employer with the freehold of 'The Laurels', indicating that the lure of property-owning was already trickling down the urban social classes.

5.   From Wilkie Collins, *Hide and Seek* (1861), as cited in Asa Briggs, *Victorian Cities* (London, 1963), 24.

2: Leasehold Development

The rapid growth of the population of London in post-medieval times led to planned residential development in the capital. During the reign of James I landowners in the area began to see the commercial advantage which could be gained from building development, for which at that time a licence from the Privy Council was required. The Council's surveyor, Inigo Jones, was involved on its behalf in the development of Lincoln's Inn Fields and in the preservation of the Fields themselves as an ornamental walk, and was required by the Council to be fully involved in a scheme by the Earl of Bedford to develop Covent Garden.[1] The subsequent civil war interrupted activity but after the Restoration those who owned land to the north and west began development in earnest and many of the names of London squares commemorate these aristocratic developers, notably Clarendon, Berkeley, Albemarle, Burlington, and Devonshire.[2]

Freehold v. leasehold
Most of this building was done on the leasehold system. The ground rents produced an enormous increase in the income of the landlords. The Duke of Bedford's Bloomsbury estate, for instance, was yielding an income of £8,000 in 1771 as against £2,000 in 1732; Lord Grosvenor's ground rents yielded £12,000 in 1802 as against £2,000 in 1722.[3] At a later date, the same situation occurred in booming provincial towns; Lord Calthorpe's income from building leases on his Edgbaston estate in Birmingham doubled from £5,233 in 1810 to £11,673 in 1845.[4]

The letting of land on building leases had several advantages. The first was financial, in that the land could be let or sublet to a builder who would be taking virtually all the risk of the development. Usually no one person was wealthy enough to take the whole risk of building a square of large houses designed to attract aristocratic or newly-rich residents. But by making the land available in lots, several builders could share the capital risk of the development, while the landowner's only risk if the development collapsed and the ground rent failed to increase was the loss of a few years' agricultural rents. Many builders went bankrupt, then as now, although some prospered; but few land owners suffered. The second advantage was that the practical benefit of control over building could be secured. If the landowner was continuing to live in the vicinity, as was normally the case in London, he could ensure that his neighbours were of the same type as himself, and that the amenities of the area were as far as possible preserved. Close control of the type of house and density of building was also advisable to maintain the value of the landlord's neighbouring land for future development. A third advantage of this arrangement, and one of great significance, was the capacity it gave landowners to preserve their estates for the future benefit of their descendants, even in those instances where the sale of the freehold title to the land was possible.

That freehold sale was often not possible was the result of the determination of landowners of former generations for whom lawyers had devised the family settlement. The usual form of settlement was created on marriage, when the families of both parties contributed to the setting up of the couple in the manner and status in society to which they had been born. The usual form of settlement gave the income of the property to the husband for life and prescribed the manner in which, after his death, with only a proportion of the income reserved for the widow, the property devolved on his descendants, normally going to the eldest son in tail, that is, on terms that made the sale of the freehold impossible. With resettlements in similar terms in every generation, dispersal of the family's landed 'power base' could be prevented. The attention given to succession of the landed estate was such that even where the estate was not settled, it was a priority of management to maintain its integrity. As a study of the Bedford and Foundling Estates notes, 'the whole day-to-day business of an estate office would be unintelligible without the assumption that the first duty of the ground landlord was to pass on to succeeding generations the value of the property unimpaired and if possible enhanced'.[5]

Settlements provided a further problem for the landlord who proposed to develop. Unless power was explicitly included in a settlement, the current beneficiary of the settlement could not grant a lease binding on his successor; hence, when he died, all leases ceased. Until 1852 the only way of altering the terms of a settlement to provide for binding leases was by private Act of Parliament, which was slow and very expensive. In practice, agricultural tenants often relied on the family feeling of the landlord to renew their leases when a son succeeded to the land. For instance, although in 1771 Sir Henry Harpur of Calke Abbey in Derbyshire obtained a private act to permit him to grant leases on his estate, little use was made of the facility, 'partly because relations between the Harpurs and their tenants-at-will were so good that (as was reported in 1806) "improvement on an extensive scale" was carried on by the latter "with as much confidence" as if they enjoyed 21-year leases'.[6]

Since no builder would invest money on terms that did not guarantee him a minimum number of years return on his investment, in 1852 the earliest of several Acts of Parliament to permit general modification of settlements was passed. These acts at first gave power to the Court of Chancery to approve the granting of binding leases; later, the Settled Land Act of 1882 specified periods for binding leases for various purposes without consent of the Court – 99 years for building, 60 years for mining, and 21 years for any other purpose.

Liverpool leaseholds
These successive Acts incidentally record the length of lease considered commercially acceptable over the greater part of the country, this being the 75-year or 99-year term that apparently developed from the 'especially ecclesiastical post-Reformation habit' of granting leases for three lives, nominated at the commencement of the lease.[7] At Liverpool, for instance, the 'three lives' system was in operation until 1712, when an additional guaranteed period of 21 years was added.[8] More than half of the area of the original township and parish of Liverpool was the property of the Corporation, thanks to the obscure annexations of the burgesses in the Middle Ages.[9] Prior to the Municipal Corporations Act of 1835, the Town Council administered this corporate estate, collecting town dues on all merchandise brought into the town by persons other than freemen, organising all markets, and – a remarkable 'improving' and entrepreneurial activity – being responsible for the building of all the earlier docks. As the dock estate grew in importance, dock dues rose from £23,380 in 1800 to nearly £200,000 in 1835 (when administration was transferred to a separate committee of the Council), providing a significant element in the booming income drawn from the Corporation's landed property.[10] While sales of land had occurred, it was generally the policy of the Council to acquire additional freeholds where possible and not to reduce its estate. Despite the different circumstances, therefore, at Liverpool as in London most of the land available for

development was offered on a leasehold basis. The system suited the
respective landlords; buildings were erected which would revert to them, with
the land, at no capital outlay on their part, and the land was meanwhile
producing an enhanced income.

The system for leasing Liverpool Corporate property in force in 1818
was described by Charles Okill and John Mercer, who on 11 December 1818
were deputed by the Council to investigate the system of registering leases,
the mode of calculating fines for renewal, and other related matters. At the
time Corporate property was leased on the three lives plus 21 years principle,
but now that the estate was so large this was proving more and more
unsatisfactory. From the landlord's point of view such a system became
increasingly difficult to administer. A large tract of land originally comprised
in one lease might become split up into hundreds of parts as streets were
formed and houses erected, so that separate leases had to be granted to the
respective tenants. As the number of leases increased, so did the difficulty of
tracing the named lives. This, and the uncertainty as to when any particular
lease would lapse, were the main grounds for changing the practice.[11] A
prospective tenant, on the other hand, might well be deterred from investing
in building by the uncertain duration of such a term, lifetimes being
problematical and only 21 years being guaranteed. Despite these difficulties,
development was sometimes undertaken. For example, in 1800 the Council
decided to develop the Moss Lake Fields in the area now covered largely by
the University of Liverpool. The land being already let, negotiations were
protracted until 1816, when the leases were surrendered; the land around
Abercromby Square was then let for three lives and 21 years (which in the
event ran to 1884) to William Lawson, merchant, and A.D. Pritt, gentlemen,
at a fine (i.e., a down payment) of 5/- and a ground rent of one penny per
annum increasing to 1/- per yard per annum when Lawson and Pritt had
erected houses.[12] An advantage of the leasehold system — especially
significant for this study — was that covenants could be imposed and enforced
to protect the amenity of the area and so maintain its desirability in the eyes
of tenants and builders alike. In the Abercromby Square area, action was
taken in 1834 and 1838 to enforce covenants against owners who allowed
cellars to be used as dwellings.[13]

While this type of development occurred in several provincial towns, in Liverpool in particular developers played a key role in land promotion.[14] During the eighteenth century the usual range of local notables, merchants, professional men and the occasional craftsman, were involved. By the early years of the nineteenth century, however, attorneys were becoming more important as channels for funds (often originating from clients with small savings): they supplied credit to craftsmen-builders with whom they worked closely. On occasions, an attorney would join with a surveyor, architect or craftsman, the attorney providing the money and handling the conveyancing, while the others laid out the ground and built roads and sewers. This pattern can be discerned in the arrangements for the park estates described later.[15] In London, in contrast, development on a much more extensive scale was undertaken by speculative builders, who calculated a commercial return on the basis of a fixed term lease. This in itself could lead to an urban environment of greater order and uniformity of style than was generally the case in the provinces, although Bath and Brighton provided notable exceptions.

Following the recommendation of the report of Okill and Mercer, from 1820 the Liverpool leasing system was changed. Lessees applying for renewals were given the option of taking a lease for 60 years, paying a fine, a capital sum, for this according to a fixed scale. The scheme was advertised and some lessees took up the offer, but since it did not prove sufficiently attractive in practice, in 1824 the term was extended to 75 years. In 1910 it was stated that this system had 'proved advantageous up to the present date' but that –

> it may not be long ere the term in Corporation leases under the sanction of Parliament or the Local Government Board, will be increased to 99 years to meet the obvious requirements of the Lessees and investors. This sanction is of course requisite because, under the Municipal Corporations Act 1882, the power of granting leases is limited to a term of 75 years.[16]

The prediction of an early change proved wrong.

Defects of the leasehold system
Clearly, where nothing else was available, as was the case in London or in
a commercial area such as the centre of the old parish of Liverpool was
becoming, leases remained acceptable. But once the wealthier citizens of the
growing industrial towns began to move out to the suburbs, they were more
interested in acquiring freeholds. 'Every man his own freeholder' heads an
1846 advertisement in the *Liverpool Mercury* for the Wirral Freeholders
Benefit Building Association, and the property advertisements in the same
newspaper displayed 'FREEHOLD' in heavy type as often as they did the
location of the property.[17]

Pressure for a reform of the leasehold system built up during the
nineteenth century. In 1883 a Leaseholders' Enfranchisement Bill was laid
before Parliament and in 1884 Lord Randolph Churchill brought forward a
second bill 'to provide for the enfranchisement of Leaseholders in Urban
Sanitary Districts': this in turn was followed in 1885 by Henry Broadhurst's
bill 'To enable Leaseholders of houses and cottages to purchase the fee
simple of their property'. The last bill was backed up by a book entitled
Leasehold Enfranchisement, one of a series of volumes on political and social
questions of the day, and this listed the iniquities of leaseholds, particularly
of the old 'three lives' type.[18] The allegedly evil effects of the leasehold
system in general were summarised as follows. It caused houses to be
cheaply and badly built, because they ultimately become the property of
someone other than the individual who built them; for the same reason it
prevented old houses being pulled down and new ones put in their place, thus
condemning families to live in houses unfit for habitation. Again, it made
occupiers grudge repairs. It placed – it was argued somewhat tendentiously
– whole towns and villages at the mercy of one or two men who could either
wholly prevent or impose any terms they pleased on the building of new
houses; and it perpetuated for a long period any restrictions however
unreasonable which had been imposed years before on the use and enjoyment
of a house. Finally – and riding a high-moral and political hobbyhorse – it
was argued that the leasehold system deprived Englishmen of that incentive
to industry and thrift offered by the prospect of acquiring a house which is
really their own, while it conferred upon landlords a degree of authority and
a right of interference in regard to the homes of the people which was

unendurable in a free country.

The desire to own freehold land was clearly strong but the law was not at that time in a position to guarantee protection of amenity. In English law, only a party to a contract can be sued for breach of that contract, but, as one of the exceptions to this rule, landlord and tenant can sue and be sued on most positive and negative covenants in a lease, whether they are the original parties to the lease or not. Thus in, say, the fortieth year of a 50-year lease, the present tenant can be sued if he is in breach of a repairing covenant, even if the landlord is a purchaser of the freehold subsequent to the lease. This exception does not apply to freeholds.

Among the 1885 complaints were many which have a presentday resonance. It was only in 1967 that the Leasehold Reform Act was passed which gave many tenants on long leases (over 21 years) the right to buy the freehold of their house. This led to the break-up of many cohesively developed and well maintained estates which had formerly been under the control of one landlord. That more damage was not done may be attributed to the Civic Amenities Act, also of 1967, which for the first time imposed a duty on local planning authorities to determine which parts of their areas were of special architectural or historical interest, therefore whose character and appearance should be preserved or enhanced. The local planning authority was required to designate such areas 'conservation areas'.

The 1967 Leasehold Reform Act applied only to houses and not flats, because the fundamental difference between leaseholds and freeholds referred to above was not then addressed. If the 1967 Act had been applied to flatted properties, it would have been impossible for owners to sue their neighbours to ensure adequate maintenance of the building. Freehold flats would thus have been liable to decline in value and would also have been refused as security by building societies. It is a matter for regret that the Leasehold Reform Housing and Urban Development Act of 1993, which enables tenants to combine to purchase the freehold of their entire building compulsorily from the landlord, still does not address this problem. Instead of simply enacting that positive covenants (that is, those requiring some action or expenditure to comply with them) should be enforceable on freeholds as they are on leaseholds, a complex scheme of buyout provisions is offered which does little more than make the tenants the managers of their own building.

Among the matters complained about in 1885 were restrictive covenants, which it was inferred were associated only with leasehold and not with freehold land. In fact, a covenant on freehold land had been enforced in the well-known case concerning Leicester Square, London, *Tulk v. Moxhay*, in 1848, and in subsequent actions.[19] (The Chancery judges of the nineteenth century thus created what is, in effect, another exception to the rule that only the parties to a contract may be liable on it.) In practice, despite the alleged disadvantages of the leasehold system, in the context of suburban development the restrictive aspects of a lease had often an advantage for the tenant. If the landlord could regulate building and enforce restrictive covenants, this was not solely to his own advantage. A discerning tenant prepared to pay a good rent would be attracted by the restrictions in the lease which protected him against interference with his comfort and amenity by other tenants of the same landlord who were subject to the same terms. Further, it was in the interests of all tenants that a vigorous estate office should oversee a uniform and enforceable regime, even on occasion leading a campaign against the intrusion of, say, tramways or canals.[20]

Restrictions on freehold
No comparable advantage could be said definitely to exist in relation to freehold land. Where a covenant was entered into between a vendor and a purchaser, it could be enforced by an action for breach of contract, but if the purchaser then sold the freehold there seems to have been continuing doubt – despite the decision in *Tulk v. Moxhay* – as to whether the original vendor could enforce the covenant, restrictive or positive, against subsequent purchasers. In any event, a freeholder did not have an estate office to complain to and act on his behalf.

It is true that restrictive covenants on freehold land had been in use since at least the late eighteenth century – their history will be considered in the following chapter.[21] However, contrasting views as to their use and effectiveness in the nineteenth century appeared in the 1889 report of the Select Committee on Town Holdings. This Committee was appointed in 1886, following the Royal Commission on the Housing of the Working Classes which sat from 1884, and also following the campaign of the Leasehold Enfranchisement Association, whose unsuccessful Bills have been mentioned above. The Report of the Select Committee commenced with a survey of the systems of tenure found in general usage at the time:

1. Freehold (that is, where freeholds were disposed of)
2. Fee farm or chief rent (that is, sale of the freehold subject to a fixed annual payment)
3. Long term leaseholds (that is, of 99-999 years)
4. Lesser term leaseholds (that is, of less than 99 years)
5. Life term leaseholds (usually for three lives)

Variations on these were found across the country. In the north of England, the four northern counties were found to be generally freehold with certain exceptions. For instance, the lands of the following owners carried the following leasehold terms: the Ecclesiastical Commissioners in Newcastle and Gateshead, 99 years; Corporation of Newcastle, 75 years; Corporation of Berwick-on-Tweed, 150 years. At Carlisle the Duke of Devonshire leased for a term of 200 years, at Workington the term was 999 years, and at Maryport there was fee farm. Yorkshire was generally freehold except in Sheffield and Huddersfield, whereas Lancashire had generally leases of 999 years in the towns, and otherwise fee farm.[22] As for Liverpool, it was mainly freehold, except for the Corporation's 75-year leases, customarily renewed on payment of a set scale of fines, and except for three large estates in the suburbs on 75-year or 99-year year leases. The Sefton and Derby estates had both adopted the Corporation practice of 75-year leases, renewable on payment of a scale of fines, while the Salisbury estate used 99-year leases. These exceptions in fact covered a substantial area of the town and its immediate vicinity.

Evidence as to the Liverpool practices was given to the Committee by Enoch Harvey, solicitor, of Liverpool, a former President of the Liverpool Law Society, who had a particular grievance stemming from the attempt by the Corporation around 1881 to increase the capital sums payable on renewal, all the Corporation land being by then built upon.[23] His detailed evidence throws light on the background to the local development of park estates. He stated that very few fee-farm rents or perpetual leaseholds were granted, though they were sometimes adopted by private landowners; they were popular with people who were not very rich. Such a rent cost a builder, for example, £40 per annum instead of £1,000 down, but it was not liked by others as it made it more difficult to get a mortgage, some mortgagees regarding a ground rent as a prior charge. When asked whether, if enfranchisement for leaseholders were available, it would not be the case that all the good property would be enfranchised and all the poor left, he replied that he did not think so –

> as nearly all the property in Liverpool is mortgaged. Liverpool is
> a borrowing place. Very few people own their own property
> without having a mortgage on it. Freehold or leasehold, a man
> considers it very bad business, he can get more out of the money
> than the interest he pays upon the mortgage.

This statement of a position so familiar in a recent period of high inflation – although no longer of uninhibited commercial speculation – had to be explained to the Committee.

Evidence in respect of other provincial towns is also relevant. George Simpson, solicitor, of Sheffield, threw some light on the way in which, in practice, restrictive covenants on freeholds were regarded at that time.[24] He stated that in Sheffield the main land landowner, the Duke of Norfolk, let on 99-year leases, as did the town trustees and the church burgesses, although about one quarter of the town was freehold. The Freehold Land Society system had been very popular in Sheffield some years previously but now had become very unpopular because of the enormous profits made by land jobbers who 'buy a plot, and float a Society, charging high to subscribers'. In Sheffield, when a freehold was conveyed a perpetual restrictive covenant could be entered into.

> Arguments are used that restrictive covenants cannot be enforced
> as well against the freeholder as against the leaseholder, but in
> answer to this, it may be said, that only a very small part of the
> property of the United Kingdom is, or ought to be, subject to
> restrictive covenants. Many of the restrictive covenants in old
> leases are practically obsolete, but until they are actually and
> legally waived, they are a source of annoyance and danger,
> although in many cases disregarded both by lessor and lessee, the
> former simply looking for his ground rent.

When asked if he thought that restrictive covenants on freeholds could be maintained, Simpson replied:

> In a reasonable way they can, but, of course, it requires a very learned man to explain the law as to covenants running with the land, starting with *Spencer's Case* and so on. But practically, there is no difficulty whatever in a large town like Sheffield. I do not know of any action being brought in consequence of a breach of a restrictive covenant, except maybe in a Land Society, or something of that sort.

What he seems to have been arguing was that restrictive covenants were not worth the trouble of imposing or defending.

Evidence in respect of Birmingham was given by William Matthews, land agent and surveyor. Much of the best property there was built and let on 99-year leases, constituting up to about three quarters of the rateable value of the town.[25] One of the main complaints under investigation being that the leasehold system offered no incentive to build soundly, Matthews went on to claim that buildings were generally a great deal better in Birmingham than in other towns. He described the process by which much of Birmingham was currently being developed (he excepted the King Edward School Estate and the prestigious Calthorpe Estate which contained 'some of the very best villas and mansions that can possibly be built'). Thus, when asked how streets and sewers were paid for, he explained as follows.

> A very common way of developing land in the suburbs of Birmingham is, for a speculator to buy a freehold property at so much per acre, he then lets it out for building and makes the streets and sewers, and leases it in lots to speculative builders at ground rents of so much per square yard. The builders erect the houses and secure the ground rents; the speculator then sells his secured ground rent to one class of investors who are content with a low rate of interest; the builders sell to investors who prefer a high rate of interest for a limited term. They repeat the process on other sites – and so buildings in Birmingham have increased very rapidly.[26]

Next, when asked about the enforcement of covenants on freehold land, Matthews replied that he had not seen any scheme for that purpose which did not seem to him to be perfectly futile.[27] Asked whether it would not be extremely expensive for a small freeholder to enforce a covenant against his neighbours – in fact such a covenant could not have existed – he replied that he did not see how one man could enforce a covenant against another. 'There is no privity of contract [even] between one leaseholder and his neighbour.'[28] Matthews was convinced of the effectiveness only of the leasehold schemes of which he had experience, where all enforcement was carried out by the landlord at the instigation of tenants offended by a breach of covenant. The landlords were willing to undertake this because, if the word got about that, as landlords, they were unwilling to perform this duty, the value of other land owned or developed by them would be undermined, certainly in the immediate neighbourhood and possibly even further afield.

It seems clear from this evidence that amenity covenants on freehold land were believed to be possible and were indeed used in some areas, but also that there was little faith in their efficacy. In its report, the Select Committee itself made no comment on their effectiveness, despite favouring – or perhaps because of favouring – freehold over leasehold development.

> The Committee, while acknowledging the advantages of building land being dealt with on a consistent plan and as a whole and the good effect which a far-seeing freeholder will exercise over the development of his property on the leasehold system, have no evidence to lead them to believe that building land is not equally laid out and developed in the large towns where the freehold system is prevalent, and the evils apprehended from every man building according to his own plan on his own freehold are, in the opinion of this Committee, to be met by the supervision of Local Authorities who should have ample powers to ensure both good building and the proper laying out of building land.[29]

The safeguard recommended by the Committee was one for the future – and as it transpired, the distant future. The country had to wait almost as long for 'Town and Country Planning' as it did for leasehold enfranchisement.

Although the 1880s was late in the history of urban development, the Select Committee could recommend no effective legal device for development regulation that interposed between, on the one hand, the potentially arbitrary control of a landlord through the leasehold system and, on the other, the complete independence of a freeholder. The widespread use of restrictive covenants over the preceding century to protect the amenity and living conditions of a freeholder disposing of part of his freehold, both for his own practical or financial benefit and for the potential benefit of his neighbours in building estates, was still, it seems, a matter of faith and hope rather than one of conviction. A body of law to uphold restrictive covenants was, however, gestating towards the end of the nineteenth century. The success of the nineteenth-century draftsmen who created the schemes as words on parchment was not fully revealed until 1957, when, in the case of *Halsall v. Brizell*, it was held that even the positive covenant requiring a contribution to the maintenance of the roads, sewers and sea wall of Cressington Park, Liverpool, was enforceable against the 1957 freeholder, although it had been imposed contractually on the purchaser of 1851.[30]

NOTES TO CHAPTER 2

1.   S. Jenkins, *Landlords to London* (London, 1975), 62.
2.   Ibid., 35 ff.
3.   Ibid., 62.
4.   D. Cannadine, *Lords and landlords: the aristocracy and the towns 1774-1967* (Leicester, 1980), 95.
5.   D. Olsen, *Town planning in London in the eighteenth and nineteenth century* (Yale, 1964), 75.
6.   H. Colvin, *Calke Abbey,Derbyshire* (London, 1985), 94.
7.   F.M.L. Thompson, 'Hampstead 1830-1914', in M.A. Simpson and T.H. Lloyd, eds, *Middle class housing in Britain* (Newton Abbott, 1977); PP 1889 XV, *Report of the Select Committee on Town Holdings*, 23: 'the shortest term has thus become prevalent as being generally the shortest term on which land can be advantageously disposed of for building'.
8.   R. Brooke, *Liverpool as it was during the last quarter of the eighteenth century 1775-1800* (Liverpool, 1853), 219.
9.   Ibid., 267.
10.   Ramsay Muir, *A history of Liverpool* (Liverpool, 1907), 263.
11.   J. Touzeau, *The rise and progress of Liverpool 1550-1835* (Liverpool, 1910), 791.
12.   Adrian Allen, 'The building of Abercromby Square', *University of Liverpool Recorder*, 95, 318.
13.   Ibid., 323.
14.   C.W. Chalkin, *The provincial towns of Georgian England* (London, 1974), 98 ff.
15.   The pattern reappeared in the 1960s and 1970s in the formation of Housing Associations, where on the principle of enlightened self-interest similar groups of professionals combined to generate work for themselves and homes for others.
16.   Touzeau, *Liverpool*, 791-2.
17.   *Liverpool Mercury*, 31 July 1846.
18.   H. Broadhurst and R.T. Reid, *Leasehold enfranchisement* (London, 1885).
19.   (1848) 2 Ph. 774. The details of this case are given in Chapter 3.
20.   Cannadine, *Lords and landlords*, 120 ff (re Edgbaston), 264 (re Eastbourne).

21.   See, e.g., *Whatman v.Gibson* (1838) 9 Sim 196, 59 ER 333, where the covenant was contained in a deed made in 1799.

22.   *Report from the Select Committee on Town Holdings* (PP 1889 XV), 6 ff.

23.   *R.S.C. Town Holdings* (PP 1888 XXII), 465-483 (Qu. 10,766-11,112).

24.   Ibid., 28 (Qu 679-1258).

25.   Ibid., 55ff (Qu 1259-1820).

26.   Ibid., 56 (Qu 1282).

27.   Ibid., 57 (Qu 1298).

28.   Ibid., 57 (Qu 1299).

29.   *R.S.C. Town Holdings*, 25.

30.   [1957] Ch 169. For a statement of the current view of positive covenants, see *Rhone v. Stephens* [1994] 2 All ER 65, where the House of Lords was invited to alter the Common Law rule but refused to do so, stressing that, to achieve this, legislation would be necessary.

3: The History of Restrictive Covenants

As we have seen, much early building development was on leasehold land, leases being the easiest way of meeting the needs of both landlords and residents. In consequence of the terms of family settlements landowners found that, without the expense of a private Act, leases were sometimes the only way of releasing land to builders. At a time when family wealth among the aristocracy tended to take the form of land rather than money, leases also avoided the need to provide the capital for a project. The covenants which were inserted in building leases, and then in the sub-leases to tenants, were designed to protect the value of land remaining in the head-landlord's hands, and to attract the higher classes of tenant, thereby securing the best rents. Good tenants would attract other good tenants and if an area became fashionable, then all concerned would be satisfied. Cannadine's 1980 account of the development of the Calthorpe estates in Edgbaston shows how well such a scheme could work over many years; it is now about 200 years since the first Lord Calthorpe made his plans and the estate is still run in a similar way.[1] An estate office deals with the day-to-day administration of the Edgbaston estate, although its former complete control is now affected by planning legislation and by the provisions of the Leasehold Reform Act of 1967, which have allowed the long-leasehold tenants of the houses on the estate to purchase the freeholds.

In contrast, Cannadine cites the example of the development of Eton College land at Chalcots, where the Provost and Fellows took no interest in the matter beyond the receipt of rents. Despite their 'inefficient and lackadaisical' administration, the builders themselves developed it as an upper-middle class area, with a high social tone. Cannadine concludes that 'given sufficient size and a favourable location, a Victorian suburban estate planned and managed itself'.[2] In social terms, where there were like-minded residents this may well have been so, but it is submitted that without a sound legal foundation the result would not have been inevitable.

A favourable location was always important, and the other conditions for success were replicated in virtually all of the nineteenth-century suburbs which continue to be desirable residential areas today. As set out in a 'rudimentary treatise' on building estates by Fowler Maitland in 1883 –

> The main features which render ground eligible for building upon
> are:– A demand for houses in the neighbourhood, proximity to a
> town, frontage to good roads, train or bus accomodation, gentle

gradients which afford facilities for drainage without making the
roads too steep, sufficient level above the sea or neighbouring
river or watercourse to ensure freedom from floods, good water
and gas supply, facilities for procuring building materials, pleasant
scenery, healthy neighbourhood and lastly, freedom from nuisance
caused by unpleasant trades or manufactures, as far as it can be
obtained without necessitating too great a distance from the scene
of business operations.[3]
From a potential tenant's or purchaser's point of view, it was easy enough
to see what was on offer at the time of first building, but in the new
circumstances of a rapidly rising population there could not be the same
certainty that a development would maintain its status over a period of time.
Although it was more usual in those days to rent than to buy a house, the
better-off were setting out to find a home that would suit them for life, and
it was unfortunate that the land law of the early nineteenth century could
offer no solution to the problems most likely to affect adversely the quality
of life in an urban or suburban society.[4]

Rights and restrictions
While the large land owners of the past had been occupied in acquiring and
preserving their estates, the necessary use of land by them and their
agricultural tenants gave rise to certain recognised types of right. When one
landowner has a legal right of some kind in respect of his neighbour's land,
this correspondingly restricts the neighbour, who is thus prevented from
acting freely on his own land in the particular regard, since this would
infringe the right. The law over the centuries has therefore been wary of
creating too wide a range of restrictive rights. The types of right most
generally recognised in the distant past were those likely to be important in
an agricultural society. Hence customs and practices emerged regarding the
use of water for domestic, irrigation and animal use; rights known as
'profits' permitted fishing, grazing, the collection of peat, wood and so on;
and 'easements' emerged. The easement was defined in *Les Termes de la
Ley*, an early legal dictionary, as 'a privilege that one neighbour hath of
another by writing or prescription without profit; as a way or sink through
his land or such like'.[5]

Despite the early recognition of these rights there was little systematic development of the law relating to easements until the nineteenth century. In the thirteenth century, Bracton had used the languages and principles of Roman law to construct a body of English law on the subject. By the eighteenth century, little had changed. Blackstone identified only 'ways or the right of going over another man's ground... [that is,] private ways in which a particular man may have an interest and a right though another may be owner of the soil.'[6] However, Blackstone did not confine easements within the parameters we now accept; the failure to distinguish clearly between various classes of right which continued from Bracton to Blackstone probably arose from the fact that all these rights were protected by the same form of legal action.[7] Writing in the early twentieth century, Holdsworth stated that such learning as was to be found on the subject of easements was generally connected with proceedings for nuisance or trespass, where there had been interference with an easement, and that gradually a clearer view had emerged of natural rights incident to ownership of land, and their distinction from easements which had to be acquired.[8]

In 1832 the Prescription Act was passed, often said to be the worst drafted piece of legislation ever, ostensibly to clarify the law, and in 1839 C.J. Gale wrote the first book to deal solely with easements. At that time there were few decided cases and many points on which there was no English authority, but with the growth of crowded cities the position soon changed. The closer individuals lived to their neighbours, the greater the pressure to acquire rights and to resist claims. The creation of water and sewage systems, gas lighting, and terraced housing all meant that householders were much more affected by their neighbours' behaviour and requirements than had been ever the case before. For instance, the closer together that dwellings and workshops huddled, the more important became rights of light. Interference with such rights generally gave rise to an action for nuisance, defined in *Les Termes de la Ley* as follows:

Nuisance is, where any man raises a wall, or stops any water, or doth any thing upon his own ground to the unlawful hurt or annoyance of his neighbour; he that is grieved may have thereof an Assise of Nusance: and if he that makes the nusance aliens the land to another, then this writ shall be brought against them both,

... It may also be by stopping lights in a house, or by causing water to run over house or lands, for remedy whereof, an action upon the Case or Assise lyeth.

During the nineteenth century the Courts gradually came to a legal conclusion regarding easements – that only a neighbouring landowner could acquire an easement, or, in other words, that for an easement to exist, there must be a dominant and a servient tenement; that for one person to impose such a restriction on another's land, the imposer must himself own an interest in land which will benefit from the right which imposes the restriction on his neighbour. This position was only stated in specific terms in 1868, and Holdsworth suggested that, as happened with so much of the common law, it had emerged from old procedural rules.[9] Actions to restrain interference with easements were founded in claims for nuisance which were available only to freeholder landowners. Be that as it may, it has also been suggested more generally that nineteenth century judges were unwilling to sanction further increases in restriction on a landowner's freedom to use his land as he chose, for example, to use it for building, where they could find a plausible basis on which to avoid it, on the unstated but assumed grounds that all restrictions tended to lower the value of the land.[10]

In respect of many of the most significant problems which the rapid growth of towns caused during the nineteenth century, it was already too late for the law of easements to offer protection. Cases had been decided from the early seventeenth century onwards which deprived the Courts of their freedom to protect those rights of privacy and certain other amenities which had come to acquire a much higher value in an urban context than they ever had in a rural one. In *William Aldred's Case* in 1611, the plaintiff complained that the defendant, Thomas Benton, had built on his orchard to the east of Aldred's land a hog-sty which obstructed the light to the plaintiff's windows, and further that the smell of the hogs corrupted the air and made the house uninhabitable. Aldred succeeded in his action on both heads; for interference with his easement of light, acquired by prescription (or long enjoyment), and for the nuisance occasioned by the smell of the hogs. Benton pleaded that the citizens of York had had a right to build as they wished since time immemorial, but Chief Justice Wray and the whole court of King's Bench, adjudging that the defence was insufficient in law, remarked:

that for stopping as well of the wholesome air, as of light, an action lies, and damages shall be recovered for them, for both are necessary ... but that for prospect, which is only a matter of delight, and not of necessity, no action lies for stopping thereof, and yet it is a great commendation of a house if it has a long and large prospect ... but the law does not give an action for such things of delight.[11]

Pursuing the notion of inactionable loss of 'delight', in *Chandler v. Thompson* in 1811 it was held that no action would lie against a landowner who built to the very extremity of his land and thus disturbed his neighbour's privacy by having windows which overlooked the latter's land. However, if, within twenty years of the original disturbance the neighbour built a wall to obstruct those windows, then this would prevent the landowner's acquisition of an easement of light and the neighbour would not be liable in nuisance.[12]

Thus, in any action for the obstruction of light, it is first necessary to prove that an easement of light actually exists and then that the obstruction of that light amounts to a nuisance, something which adversely affects a landowner in the use and enjoyment of his land or of an easement from which his land benefits. Where a right of light does exist, it will only prevent a neighbour from committing a nuisance. As Farwell J. said, in *Higgins v. Betts*:

> It is still, as it always has been, a question of nuisance or no nuisance, but the test of nuisance is not – How much light has been taken, and is that enough materially to lessen the enjoyment and use of the house which its owner previously had? but – How much is left, and is that enough for the comfortable use and enjoyment of the house according to the ordinary notions of mankind?[13]

Actions for nuisance can mitigate unpleasantness but are not able to create or preserve pleasant surroundings or attractive views or a secluded dwelling. A landowner cannot ensure privacy or an uninterrupted view. To quote Scott L.J. in *McVittie v. Bolton Corporation*: 'English law had long recognised the duty of occupiers of land not to offend their neighbour's sense of smell or hearing, but had left them lamentably free to offend their neighbour's sense of sight.'[14] Thus, one may impose on one's neighbours anything which the 'ordinary, reasonable' man or woman would find acceptable, a bottom-line test, since what is ordinarily reasonable may not be what some sensitive individuals or groups regard as acceptable.

Covenants recognized and defined

Wealthy refugees from the nineteenth-century inner-city areas were aiming to rise above the standards of living of the ordinary man or woman and hence did not accept this limitation of nuisance. In view of the restricted protection offered by the common law, in order to protect their suburban sensibilities they had recourse to the law of contract. Despite the disadvantages of the leasehold system set out in Chapter 2 above, particularly in relation to unplanned development, the peculiar advantage of leasehold was that not only were covenants in a lease enforceable in contract between landlord and tenant, but that covenants 'touching and concerning' the land were also enforceable between subsequent owners of both the freehold and of the leasehold interests in the land. In other words, such covenants are said to 'run with the land', meaning that the liability will pass beyond the original contracting parties.

While the rules governing the relationship of landlord and tenant were clear and well understood, the same could not be said of covenants imposed on the sale of a freehold. As noted in Chapter 2, in the early 1830s a thorough review of property law was undertaken by a Commission set up 'to inquire into the Law of England respecting real property'. Reporting in 1832, the Commissioners found the law to be very uncertain and made various recommendations.[15] Some of these were put into effect by decisions of the Chancery Court in subsequent cases, while others were only acted upon statutorily in 1925. It must be borne in mind that one object of the conveyancers who draft the documents by which transactions are effected is to avoid appearing before the courts; consequently, cases recording, registering, and in that sense legitimising a procedure are likely to occur long after a particular conveyancing habit has been established as normal practice. For example, one of the 1832 comments was that 'it is a sound maxim that he who takes the benefit ought also to bear the burthen'; this was the principle used to decide the case of *Halsall v. Brizell* in 1957, 125 years after the report, although it is doubtful if even the judge was aware of the historical background.[16] Several subsequent commentators have mistakenly regarded his use of the maxim as novel.

The views of the Commission regarding the contemporary status of covenants are of considerable significance. After an analysis of the state of the law, as understood at the time, with regard to covenants in general and in the context of leases, the Commissioners turned to the law regarding freeholds. The effect of certain types of covenants in freehold conveyances was clear, but in the case of 'covenants made by the owner of land to which they relate' considerable uncertainty was found to be the case. The Report dealt only with the burden of such covenants which

> have relation to interest possessed or acquired by the covenantee, independently of the covenant; such as a covenant to pay a rent-charge issuing out of the land, or to maintain a road over it; others are not connected with any such interests in the land, as a covenant by the owner of a particular close, that it shall never be built on, but will always remain an open space. We shall consider these separately, though the alterations we have to propose will apply equally to both.

The building schemes to be considered later contained covenants of both the types noted above, that is, positive covenants to maintain roads (positive, because compliance involve expenditure), and negative covenants restricting building (where compliance involves no expense). The law on the enforceability of these covenants when the land had passed from the original covenanting owner was at this date not settled:

> Whether the burthen of such covenants, of either description, runs with the land, so that an action of covenant at law can be maintained against an alienee, seems to have been lately questioned.

It may be inferred that concern about these unsettled issues was a recent development.

Turning to what we now call restrictive covenants, the Commissioners stated that, 'in modern times' (i.e., from the sixteenth century up to 1832), such covenants were frequently found where the areas of squares or public walks were to be preserved, or where an uninterrupted view of the sea or of open country was to be preserved.

Doubts, nevertheless, appear to have been extensively entertained both as to the efficacy of such covenants for the purposes they are intended to answer, and as to their validity. With respect to the former, the principal ground of doubt has been, whether they would run with the land so as to bind all successive owners of it. Judged by the usual rule, (and supposing the usual rule to be applicable), perhaps this doubt may be thought to be unfounded, for they relate directly and immediately to the land. If such a covenant is not binding, at least in equity, on an assignee of the land, [then] a title to property, the enjoyment of which materially depends upon it, must obviously be defective. It does not very clearly appear under what impression as to their effect such covenants have been introduced or sanctioned by practitioners; probably they have seldom been viewed as creating at law any other than a personal obligation. We are not aware of any instance in which an action at law upon such a covenant has been brought against an assignee of the land referred to in it. In a few cases the subject has been brought before the Court of Equity by suit against an assignee of the land; in some of these cases, the Court has refused to interfere by way of injunction, but the validity of the covenant, or its binding the assignee, has never been negatived by any decision.

This was hardly a satisfactory situation.

The report went on to note that, despite the use of various legal devices which in theory might solve the problem, in instances where the property was of sufficient value to bear the expense, a private Act of Parliament was the safest solution. 'These covenants being thus of frequent occurrence, and of great importance', the Commissioners recommended that a general register listing them should be established. This would remove the objection that the existence of covenants might not be known to purchasers. An alternative possibility open to the Commmission, that of declaring that such covenants were merely personal (presumably precluding even the assistance of a court of equity), 'would be almost entirely to destroy the use of them; for in that case, the benefit would scarcely survive the generation in which the covenant was created'.[17]

The preferred solution of the Commission was to permit enforcement in equity, the suitable remedy being specific performance.[18] Only in the Chancery Court could proper weight be given to the lack of prior notice of the existence of a covenant. If it should appear that a purchaser for valuable consideration was a purchaser without notice (that is, one who was unaware of the covenant at the time of purchase) and there was no negligence on his part, the court would refuse to order observance of the covenant. However, if a register were to be established, this would not often occur. Similarly,

if it should appear that the covenant was originally inconvenient and contrary to public policy, either as going beyond the necessity of the case in the quantity of the land covered by it, or in the nature of the restrictions imposed, or that, although not in the first instance open to any such objection, it had subsequently become inconvenient and objectionable on grounds of public policy, in either case the court would be at liberty to refuse its interference.

The proposed register was not in fact set up until 1 January 1926. But it is striking to see how far, through cases, the law developed in accordance with the recommendations of this report.

In 1832 the Commissioners noted that they had only 'a few cases before courts of equity' to look to for guidance. One of these was probably the *Duke of Bedford v. The Trustees of the British Museum* (1822).[19] By a settlement of 1669, on the marriage of Lady Rachel Vaughan and Lord Russell, Southampton House and adjoining fields in Bloomsbury were conveyed to trustees. Part of this land (over seven acres) was sold in 1675 for £2,600, plus a rent of £5 per annum, to Ralph Montagu, his heirs and assigns, subject to a covenant with Lady Vaughan, her heirs and assigns, that only one 'fair and large mansion' with outbuildings would be erected on the land, and that if there was a breach of this condition, Montagu, his heirs and assigns would pay Lady Vaughan, her heirs and assigns, £3 per day until compliance was restored. A mansion was built, burnt down and replaced. Soon after the establishment of the British Museum, Montagu House was purchased and vested in trustees for the institution. Meanwhile, Southampton House, renamed Bedford House, and the remaining land had been purchased by the Duke of Bedford, who collected the £5 rent per annum. Bedford House itself was pulled down in 1800 to make way for streets and buildings on the site, including on the north, east and west sides of the Museum, some overlooking its gardens. When the Museum sought to build an extension to house the Elgin Marbles, the Duke of Bedford applied for an injunction to restrain this breach of the 1675 covenant. The case came in 1822 before the Lord Chancellor, Lord Eldon, assisted by the Master of the Rolls. In 1839 Samuel Atkinson summarised the judgement thus:

> [Eldon] was of the opinion that the character of the adjoining land had been so altered with reference to the land conveyed, that the restriction in the covenant had ceased to be applicable according to the intent and spirit of the contract; that a court of equity would not interpose to enforce the covenant but would leave the parties to their remedy at law; but whether the parties had any remedy at law, was a point upon which both judges carefully abstained from giving any opinion.[20]

Several cases were cited in the judgement bearing on the question of whether it was necessary to show a legal right before an equitable remedy could be granted, but no decision was made on the point.

Other cases with a bearing – or possible bearing – on the efficacy of covenants prior to the 1832 Report included *Roper v. Williams*, also heard in 1822 by Lord Eldon. Williams had conveyed to Roper land adjoined on three sides by other land owned by the former. Williams had therefore covenanted that he, his heirs and asssigns, would not at any time thereafter erect or suffer to be erected on the land on the north side of the ground conveyed, any buildings whatsoever; and further that all buildings to be erected by him, his heirs, appointees and assigns or any person or persons claiming under him or them, on the land on the east or west sides should be built 30 feet from the intended road, and that these buildings should be detached houses of not less than the third rate or class of building. Later Williams contracted to sell to B, another defendant, and was about to convey without requiring a similar covenant from the purchaser, while B had agreed to let to M for the building of houses inferior to the covenant specification and differently situated. M commenced building; Roper obtained an injunction. On appeal the Vice-Chancellor refused to dissolve the injunction, but when appeal was made to the Lord Chancellor, he did dissolve it. It appeared that, at an earlier date, Roper had served B with a notice requiring him not to proceed with the erection of houses which did not conform to the covenant, 'but that on being shown the opinion of counsel that the rights under the covenant could not be insisted upon, the plaintiff had taken no steps to enforce the notice, and had permitted the defendant to complete the buildings'. Lord Eldon dissolved the injunction on the grounds that the plaintiff had acquiesced in the building, saying that 'the courts of equity will not interfere unless the most active diligence has been exerted throughout the whole proceedings'.[21]

Rankin v. Huskisson is also of some interest.[22] In this case, heard in 1830 by the Vice-Chancellor, Sir Lancelot Shadwell, an injunction was granted against the Commissioners of Woods restraining them from building on the site of Carlton Palace, in violation of a term of an agreement with the plaintiffs for a 99-year building lease of an adjoining part of the site. Having entered into an agreement that the ground on the south side of that to be leased to the United Services Club should be laid out as an ornamental garden and that no buildings whatsoever should be erected thereon, the Commissioners subsequently entered into agreements with Huskisson and Lawley for the building of stables on this land. The clubhouse had already been built and the stables were so close to it as to exclude light and air from it. The bill sought specific performance of the agreement with the Commissioners; while no question arose of assignment or the running of the covenant, the order made by the Vice-Chancellor not only restrained continuation of building but also required removal of the stables so far erected – an early example of a 'mandatory' injunction, one which requires something to be done rather than merely preventing further activity.

What was clear to the Commissioners of 1832 was that, for many years, conveyancers had been drafting building schemes on sales of freehold land which contained covenants, most of them restrictive in substance (although the courts had not so far made explicit a distinction between positive and negative covenants). No-one was sure as to the precise legal effect of such covenants. Whether it was because legal advisors were emboldened by the support of the Report of the Real Property Commissioners, or because of the passing of a 'generation' since schemes had become popular (as noted in the Report), or by mere coincidence, it was not long before courts found cases in front of them which gave judges the opportunity of putting into effect the suggestions of the Commissioners.

The views of Lord Brougham were offered on some points soon after the 1832 publication. In 1834, as Lord Chancellor, he heard an application to dissolve an injunction in the case of *Keppell v. Bailey*. The covenant in question was a commercial one and so not directly comparable to those found in building schemes but an argument advanced in favour of enforcing the covenant was that the assignees, Messrs. Bailey, had had notice of it. On this point, the *Third Report of the Real Property Commissioners* was one of the authorities cited to the Court, but the argument was decisively rejected by the Lord Chancellor:

> The knowledge by an assignee of an estate, that his assignor had assumed to bind others than the law authorises him to affect by his contracts — had attempted to create a real burthen upon property, which is inconsistent with the nature of that property, and unknown to the principles of the law, cannot bind such assignee by affecting his conscience. If it did, then the illegality would be of no consequence; and however wild the attempt might be to create new kinds of holding and new species of estate, and however repugnant such devices might be to the rules of law, they would prove perfectly successful in the result, because equity would enable their authors to prevail; nay, not only to compass their object, but to obtain a great deal more than they could at law, were their contrivances ever so accordant with legal principle. This Court would be occupied in compelling persons by way of injunction and decree to perform covenants which the law repudiated, and for the breach of which no damages could ever be recovered.[23]

This extreme view of the danger of enforcing covenants in equity ignored the stated caveat of the Commissioners' report which said that if the court felt that a covenant was not in the public interest, then it would be at liberty to refuse an injunction.

In 1838 Cottenham replaced Brougham as Lord Chancellor and *Whatman v. Gibson* came before Shadwell V.C. This case concerned a row of houses on a two-and-a-half acre plot in Ramsgate made the subject of a mutual deed of covenant in 1799. It is thus one of the earliest of the building schemes litigated in the nineteenth century.[24] The deed was entered into between the landowner, two freehold purchasers, their heirs, executors, administrators and assigns who had already agreed to buy, and the several other persons who should at any time execute the deed. It contained covenants restricting the use to 'good dwelling-houses or lodging-houses' only, and also covenants to maintain the unity of building appearance, and to maintain the road and footpath in front of the house. It was thus very similar to the Liverpool schemes discussed later and probably to most other schemes. In 1802 house number 7 of the row was sold subject to the covenants to A who signed the deed, and then, through other sales, it came into the hands of Gibson, who leased it to Gomm who opened it as the Royal Victoria Hotel. Whatman had purchased the neighbouring house, number 6, from C in 1818, subject to the covenants, C having purchased from the original landowner in 1800, and he objected to the hotel. Gomm admitted that he knew of the deed of 1799, but insisted that he ought not to be affected by it. It was held that, as there was a clear breach of the covenant, the only question was:

> whether, there being an agreement, all persons who come in as devisees or assignees under those who took with notice of the deed are not bound by it. I see no reason why such an agreement should not be binding in equity on the parties so coming in with notice.

The Vice-Chancellor concluded that each proprietor had an interest in preserving the general character of the row and thus maintaining the value of his property, and that, whatever the form of the covenant or the difficulty of bringing an action on it, there was a plain agreement which a court of equity ought to enforce.[25]

Another case involving a deed of mutual covenant arose in 1839. *Schreiber v. Creed* concerned a building development in Cheltenham pursuant to a deed of 1827 made between Pitt, the landowner, and the other persons who had executed the deed. A plan was annexed to the deed, which contemplated the establishment of a spa, with a pump room at the north end of the land, gardens, walks, other facilities, and building plots. Pitt reserved the right to vary details of the scheme and no injunction was in fact granted to a sub-purchaser, Schreiber. But in the course of his judgment, Shadwell V.C. said that it was quite plain −

that a mode of dealing with the land which would go directly to destroy those lawns, promenades etc., never could be permitted; because any one of the persons parties to the deed might have a remedy, as well by action of covenant as by bill in equity, to restrain Pitt his heirs or assigns from any general dealing with the land which would have the effect of destroying those promenades and plantations.[26]
Thus the judges were edging towards more settled and clearer views.

Writing in 1844, George Sweet quoted extensively from the 1832 Report and, in the light of cases heard since its publication, found that the law on covenants remained unsatisfactory; but he concluded that the obligation of a covenant with the owners of lands not to use adjoining lands in a specific manner may indeed bind the assignee.[27] In the same year, in *Bristow v. Wood*, the possible enforceability of covenants not to build houses of a less value than £300 or to carry on any trade or business on certain land near Liverpool was raised as a ground for avoiding a purchase of part of the land, and the argument was accepted, Knight-Bruce V.C. being of the opinion that the question was of too doubtful a nature to compel the purchaser to accept the title. In 1846, in *Mann v. Stephens*, Shadwell V.C. granted an injunction to prevent breach of a covenant not to open a beer-shop in circumstances where there had been notice and this injunction was confirmed by Lord Cottenham on appeal.[28]

By 1848, therefore, there were already several cases which might have given their name to the evolving rules regarding covenants. But instead, perhaps on the common principle that an event concerning London outweighs several similar ones in the provinces, it was the case of *Tulk v. Moxhay*, heard on appeal by Lord Cottenham, which became famous among property lawyers. *Tulk v. Moxhay* is now generally taken as the case which first formally set out the principles by which a covenant may run with the land in equity. Writing in 1909, W.A. Jolly summarised developments thereafter:

The doctrine [in *Tulk v. Moxhay*] never received any countenance from Lord Eldon; neither Vice-Chancellor Shadwell, who was the first to enforce it, nor Lord Cottenham, who first stated it in an authoritative form, ever attempted to support it upon any logical principle. Sir George Jessel simply accepted it as he found it, and defined its operation in a manner now generally approved. Some judges, such as Lord Romilly, maintained that the burden of the covenant ran with the land at law ... Others, such as Lord Justice Cotton, considered that the burden rested on the conscience of the purchaser ... The explanation of the doctrine given by Lord St. Leonards is really based on the assumption that the jurisdiction of equity to enforce a negative stipulation by injunction was equivalent to specific performance ...[29]

Confusion as to the origin of legal rules may arise because practising lawyers are naturally concerned more with the outcome of their current case rather than with history. *Tulk v. Moxhay* may be convincingly viewed as the culmination of a process whereby the recommendations of the Real Property Commissioners received judicial approval. Logic and principle were not at the centre of the Commissioners' arguments; rather, the Commissioners were concerned that business efficacy should be given to long-standing practical arrangements, repudiation of which which might materially affect the value of land benefitted by such covenants. In its usual pragmatic way, English law responded to this evident commercial reality and found a way of achieving the necessary protection.

The case itself concerned Leicester Square. Tulk owned the freehold of the vacant land in the centre of the Square. He sold it to Elms who covenanted for himself, his heirs and assigns, that he would 'keep and maintain the said piece of ground and Square Garden, and the iron railing round the same, in its then form, and in sufficient and proper repair as a Square Garden and Pleasure Ground, in an open state, uncovered with any buildings'. The land came into the hands of Moxhay, who admitted that he took the land with notice of the covenant, yet proposed to build on the square. Tulk still owned several houses round the square and obtained an injunction to prevent the building. Attention was not given to the positive aspect of the covenant which required the owner to keep the garden in proper and sufficient repair.[30]

Application of covenants to building schemes

After *Tulk v. Moxhay*, decisions tended to limit the scope of its *ratio* (the legal principle on which a decision is based), lest too many novel restrictions be placed on land, of a kind previously unknown to the law. It was not settled until 1881 that only negative covenants would be enforced by equity, or until 1882, that equity would enforce a restrictive covenant only if it was taken originally for the protection of other land.[31] Even at the end of the century a well-respected writer could comment:

> But the whole principle of *Tulk v. Moxhay* rests on the dubious grounds of equity, and it seems in the courts below, to have been carried to some absurd lengths. It has never been considered by the House of Lords; and it is not improbably destined ... to have its wings clipped whenever it shall come before that august tribunal.[32]

However, by the time of the preparation of the property legislation eventually passed in 1925, the principle had gained so much ground that restrictive covenants were accepted as being interests in land which should be protected by registration, as first proposed in 1832.

Almost all of the early cases concern building schemes; as more cases came before the courts, more detail was added to the principles and to the occasions on which equity would enforce covenants. The restrictions were generally in line with the Commissioners' views on the granting of injunctions, but some of the rules came too late to affect building schemes themselves, many of which were begun before the report. Despite the long period of use of such schemes in one form or another, the essential elements are now accepted as having been most clearly set out in *Elliston v. Reacher* (1908): that both plaintiff and defendant must derive title from a common vendor; that the common vendor must have laid out the land in lots for building, subject to restrictions intended to apply to all purchasers; that the lots must have been bought from him on that footing; and that the area to which the scheme applies must be clearly defined.[33]

The case itself concerned land in Felixstowe bought in 1860 by the Conservative Land Society. A plan was prepared, and the estate was lotted and conditions drawn up subject to which the lots were to be sold. In 1861 the estate was conveyed to trustees for the building society and a deed was prepared, pursuant to the conditions of sale, for signature by the trustees and all purchasers. The deed contained covenants by the purchasers with each other and with the trustees, to observe the restrictions contained in the deed. Despite being prepared, dated and stamped, the deed was never signed by any party. Nevertheless the Society's printed form of conveyance contained a covenant by each purchaser to observe the covenants contained in the 1861 deed. It was held that a general building scheme existed in this case, according to the principles set out above, despite the fact that the intended deed of mutual covenant had never been executed. The scheme appears to resemble closely the Liverpool schemes, save that in those schemes the deeds of covenant were executed.

The requirements set out in *Elliston v. Reacher* were so strictly applied thereafter that there appear to be only two reported cases between 1908 and 1965 in which a building scheme was successfully claimed (other than *Halsall v. Brizell* noted in Chapter 2).[34] Since 1965, however, there has been a change of attitude on the part of the judiciary, which now appears much more willing to concede that the benefits of such schemes should be recognised. By this means, many Victorian residential areas may have been preserved from the developers of the 1960s and 1970s, even before the statutory protection of Conservation Areas became available.

NOTES TO CHAPTER 3

1.   See D. Cannadine, *Lords and landlords: the aristocracy and the towns 1774-1967* (Leicester, 1980).

2.   Ibid., 399.

3.   F. Maitland, *Building estates - a rudimentary treatise on the development, sale, purchase and general management of building land* (London, 1883), 7.

4.   Somewhat lower down the social scale, Mr Pooter wished to reside in 'The Laurels', Brickfield Road, for life, as he told his employer when the latter wished to reward him: 'I love my house and I love the neighbourhood and I never wish to leave it.'

5.   *Les Termes de la Ley*, 1721 edition, 284. The original version was ascribed by Sir Edward Coke (Lord Chief Justice) to William Rastell (fl. c.1560), 'as zealous a Romanist as his uncle, Sir Thomas More'.

6.   William Blackstone, *Commentaries on the Laws of England*, 8th ed. (London, 1765), Bk II, 35. Blackstone was Solicitor General and his Commentaries were 'the substance of a course of lectures on the laws of England, which were read by the author in the University of Oxford' in 1753, the first lectures on the subject to be given in an English university.

7.   A.W.B. Simpson, *An introduction to the history of the land law* (Oxford, 1961), 108.

8.   W.S. Holdsworth, *A history of English law*, 14 vols (London, 1903), 3: 154.

9.   *Rangeley v. Midland Railway Company* (1868), 3 Ch. App., 306.

10.   M.F.Sturley, 'Easements in gross', *Law Quarterly Review*, 96, 1980, 557-67.

11.   (1611) 9 Co. Rep. 57b.

12.   (1811) 3 Camp. 80.

13.   [1905] 2 Ch 210 at 215.

14.   [1945] KB 281 at 283.

15.   *Third Report of the Real Property Commissioners* (PP 1832 (484)), XXIII, 321.

16.   [1957] Ch 169.

17.   *Third Report of the Real Property Commissioners*, 55.

18.   The main court of equity was the Court of Chancery made infamous by Dickens for its delays in handling certain types of case. It was however, in earlier times, noted for its invention of new remedies and in general for being more flexible and responsive than the common law courts such as King's/Queen's Bench.

19.   (1822) 2 My & K 552; 39 ER 1055.

20.   S. Atkinson, *The theory and practice of conveyancing* (2nd ed., London, 1839), 2 vols, 1: 447.

21.   (1822) Turn & R 18; 37 ER 999.

22.   (1830) 4 Sim 13; 58 ER 6.

23.   (1834) 2 My & K 517; 39 ER 1042.

24.   *Sheppard v. Gilmore* (1887) 57 Law J. Rep. Chanc. 6 - concerns schemes in Bath dating from 1776-1788.

25.   (1838) 9 Sim 196; 59 ER 333.

26.   (1844) 1 Coll 480; 63 ER 508

27.   G. Sweet, ed., *Bythewood and Jarman's system of conveyancing*, 3rd ed., 2 vols (London, 1844), 354.

28.   (1846) 15 Sim 377; 60 ER 665.

29.   W.A. Jolly, *Restrictive covenants affecting land* (London, 1909), 2.

30.   (1848) 2 Ph 774; 41 ER 1143.

31.   *Haywood v. Brunswick Permanent Benefit Building Society* (1881), 8 QBD 403; *London and South West Railway v Gomm* (1882) 20 Ch D 562.

32.   H.W. Challis, *The law of real property* (London, 1885), 151; 2nd ed. (1890), 173.

33.   [1908] 2 Ch 655.

34.   *Newman v. Real Estate Property Corporation* [1940] 1 All E R 131; *Bell v. Norman C. Ashton Ltd.* (1956) 7 P & CR 359.

4: Covenant-based Building Schemes

In the course of the nineteenth century, covenanted building schemes emerged in two basic forms: (a) those where a single vendor sold off portions of an estate subject to the same or similar covenants in order to maintain the value of retained land, and (b) those where a group of individuals purchased land, generally to build houses for their personal occupation, the covenants being imposed by themselves in order to maintain the amenity and residential character of the estate. In general this latter type seems to have been the more successful, in that instances can still be found operating as originally envisaged. This type in turn took two forms. The schemes at Liverpool which are examined below – and probably some of the others elsewhere – appear to have had limited profit motive behind them, although directed by other aspects of 'enlightened self interest'. But from evidence to the 1889 Select Committee on Town Holdings it seems that in some localities speculators bought land with the object of promoting a freehold land society to which they could then sell the land for covenanted building at a substantial profit. It was alleged that in Sheffield this procedure had to a large extent discouraged purchasers from freehold purchase.

Despite doubts about the efficacy of covenants against assignees of freehold land, schemes continued to be introduced and operated without the legal formalities followed in the early days. Eventually, therefore, there was pressure for the formulation of rules to introduce some consistency into litigation and legal decisions. It is submitted, not that it is remarkable that early schemes were successful in anticipating the rules finally settled on in *Elliston v. Reacher*, but that this was inevitable, given that the rules themselves emerged from the context and practice of the older schemes.

Statutory building schemes

It was noted in the Third Report of the Real Property Commissioners in 1832 that, at that time, if the value of the land would bear the expense an Act of Parliament was the advised and accepted way of creating a covenant scheme. Probably the best-documented example of this is Victoria Park in Manchester. Its political and administrative history was examined in 1976 by Spiers.[1] The 'scheme' for Victoria Park was advertised in 1836; about 180 acres was to be purchased, and within this area an ornamental park was to be laid out with plots for mansion and villa residences for sale or letting. Eight landowners and merchants agreed to promote a company and to obtain an Act of Parliament to establish the legal status of the scheme. By an Act of 5 May 1837 the Victoria Park Company was granted corporate status as a company to be run on the principle of a tontine, where the survivor of the nominated lives takes the property.[2] Each shareholder was to nominate a 'life'; if this life dropped within the three years during which shares were to be issued another life could be nominated. But after the three years, and once the number of surviving lives had been reduced to fifty, the shareholders represented by these fifty lives were to become absolutely entitled to the capital and property of the Company.[3] Section 15 of the Act gave the Company power to purchase land on chief rents and set out the form of conveyance to be used for this. Section 17 gave the power to enter into contracts for the forming of the Park and the construction of private residences, one or more churches, lodges and gates, and also other buildings for public purposes (but not trade). The proprietors agreed to pay their proportionate parts of the maximum sum of £500,000, and further agreed that they would from time to time pay a due and just proportion of the money required for making and maintaining the works.

The 1837 Act did not specify the form of conveyance or lease to proprietors; Section 94 gave the power to sell either for a gross sum or on rent charges, and Section 96 gave the power to lease for any term of years or lives as the Company or the directors thought fit. Assuming the body corporate to continue for a reasonable length of time, there was (theoretically) no problem in enforcing the covenants. The original vendor/lessor (the 'Company') would be enforcing covenants against shareholders who, on buying their share, had bound themselves to act in accordance with the company's regulations. Most of the sections of the Act were in fact concerned with the 'articles of association' of the Company rather than with the actual building scheme. In practice, the insertion of covenants in conveyances and leases seems to have been rather haphazard, as also was, apparently, the keeping of records. In 1898, when a dispute arose with Sir William Anson concerning the 'building tie', counsel's opinion had to be sought.[4] Anson proposed to build cottages (or to sell land for them) on land which he had inherited within the area of the company. One resident claimed that 'the property on which his land was built had been purchased on the condition that the land behind it should not be built upon except with a tie of £40'. The Park committee was reduced to declaring that 'additional enquiries from various people were necessary to see if it was possible to find someone who could directly allege that he bought his land on the express undertaking that the adjoining land was not to be built upon except with a tie'.[5] By 1898, therefore, these covenants were already difficult to maintain.

Much earlier the Company had itself failed. When its problems became apparent, this gave rise in 1834 to a well-known case in company law, that of *Foss v. Harbottle*.[6] Foss and Turton, on behalf of themselves and all other shareholders except the defendants, brought an action against the five remaining directors of the Company (three of whom had become bankrupt), a proprietor who was not a director, and the solicitor and architect of the Company, alleging various fraudulent and illegal transactions. The action failed on the ground that the Company's constitution could itself be used to effect a remedy, by the shareholders voting for the dismissal and replacement of the existing directors, their successors then being able to bring an action on behalf of the Company. The Company finally faded away in the trade depression of 1838 and following years. It disposed of its assets as well as it could, in most cases land as yet unsold being reconveyed to the original owners. As a result of the failure, in 1845 a meeting of residents was called and the Victoria Park Trust formed, with the object of preserving the amenity and privacy of the park. Despite the difficulties which arose because the trust did not have the legal powers which the Act had conferred on the Company, the Trust Committee continued in existence until the early 1950s, by which time the nature of the area surrounding the park had changed radically. Manchester had surrounded and absorbed the district and most of the mansions in the park were being used for non-residential purposes. Tolls had been imposed on the park roads to prevent passing traffic – as they were at Sandfield Park in Liverpool[7] – and the Trustees had attempted over the years to supplement these tolls with a 'Park rate' assessed on the general rate basis but as a voluntary addition to it. Spiers comments that 'there could have been no compulsion on residents and occupiers to pay those rates and contribution was very much a voluntary affair, depending on personal relations and contracts'. Inevitably, the expense of maintaining the sewerage, roads, lighting and other communal facilities was beyond the trust and responsibility was finally handed over to Manchester Corporation. As for the 1880s dispute with Anson, this was compromised, and the question of whether the covenants taken over by the trust were legally binding was never tested in court. Although there does not seem to have been a consistent or well-known set of covenants, the intention of the covenanting is clear.

A more recent example of an Act of Parliament obtained to confirm the efficacy of a covenant scheme is the Wentworth Estate Act of 1964. This act 'to make provision for the maintenance of the private roads and footpaths on the estate known as the Wentworth Estate' in Egham and Bagshot, Surrey, was passed in order to transfer the continuing management of the private residential estate (near the famous golf club) from the original company, W.G.Tarrant Limited, taken over in 1943 by Sir Lindsay Parkinson and Company Limited, to a new incorporated company, The Wentworth Estate Roads Committee. The Act recites that 'at a later date doubts arose as to the enforceability of some of the covenants against successors in title of the original purchasers and in some cases payments required by the covenants have not been paid'. By Section 14 of the act, the Committee was empowered to levy a rate on a new uniform basis and to enforce any covenant by the purchaser in an original conveyance and also on certain hitherto 'unchargeable hereditaments' as the earlier company had had power to do. In *Re Henman's Application* (1970), the Committee was successful in resisting an application to the Lands Tribunal − one of the first to be heard following the amendment of Section 84 of the Law of Property Act of 1925 − for the modification of the covenants to permit the building of a second house on what was originally a single plot, though by then subdivided.[8]

Building schemes by mutual covenant
The alternative method by which early schemes were created was by the execution of mutual deeds of covenant. Some cases have already been referred to, and this was the method in the case of the three Liverpool schemes whose history is examined in the following chapters. In 1909 Jolly stated that these deeds were generally entered into by the owner of the estate laid out for building, by two or three named purchasers, and by the several persons who should at any time execute the indenture (in a similar manner deeds of arrangement are executed by creditors who accede to them).[9] The

subsequent execution was important before the passing of the 1844 Act 'to Simplify the Transfer of Property'[10]. Section 11 of this Act permitted a party who had not signed a deed nevertheless to claim a benefit under it. The method might be used either by a single vendor imposing a scheme on land which he had decided to develop, or by a group of individuals who bought land for their own benefit and on which they created their own scheme. The instances which might be described as successful, in that they have survived to the present day, are of this latter type. Apart from the vendors and purchasers of lots, trustees were also parties to the original deeds. This was so that they could be responsible for the protection of purchasers, and also so that they could hold land not sold to plot owners, for example, in the Liverpool schemes, the roads, sewers and the promenade.

It has proved difficult to trace schemes in localities other than Liverpool but a case in 1986 drew attention to three other continuing schemes near Newcastle upon Tyne. The case, *Price and another v. Bouch and others*, concerned the Painshaw Field, Batt House and Birches Nook Estate, together generally known as the Stocksfield Estate, set up by a deed of mutual covenant of 30 May 1895.[11] The two other estates recorded during the case were the Darras Hall Estate and the Axwell Park Estate, whose deeds are dated 1 November 1910 and 21 November 1923 respectively. These three active schemes demonstate a late flowering of the deed of mutual covenant. No doubt there are other such schemes elsewhere but their members appear to be keeping their business to themselves in traditional manner. If the Law Commission's proposal for the reform of restrictive covenants is ever acted upon and a register of covenants in building schemes is established, it will be possible to find other active schemes and attempt a wider survey of their significance. The history of the establishment of the Newcastle schemes is, however, not without interest.

The Trustee of the Stocksfield Estate, to whom unsold land was conveyed 'for convenience', was Joseph Whiteside Wakinshaw of Runnymeade, Kenton, Northumberland, cashier.[12] Wakinshaw was also one of the trustees of Darras Hall Estate, the other two being Hugh Morton, gentleman, and Frederick Emley, solicitor. Multiple purchase of lots on these estates was a common practice. The 174 lots at Stocksfield were divided between fifty-three tradesmen; of the total Wakinshaw signed for ten. At

Darras Hall, a large estate of 925 acres in 185 lots (as appears from the first schedule to the trust deed), Wakinshaw agreed to take ten acres as did a spinster Wakinshaw of the same address; another seven were taken by another spinster Wakinshaw (same address) and five by a William Wakinshaw, a Wesleyan minister with a London address. At this estate, £14 per acre was contributed (making a total of £12,876) and a further £12,000 was advanced on an equitable charge of the property. The Rev. William Wakinshaw re-appears as the first signatory of the Deed of Mutual Covenant of the Axwell Building Estate and is the first named of the seven committee members appointed by the deed from the fourteen original covenantors. The plan shows 133 lots on an area of approximately 322 acres. Each house plot was to have been at least 500 square yards and a substantial area was allotted to a recreation ground. No flats were to be erected, nor was any trade or business permitted, including (as nuisance or annoyance) a gaol, inebriate home, or asylum for idiots, lunatics or feeble-minded persons.

In *Price v. Bouch*, the developers, the Prices, had been refused approval by the Committee of the Stocksfield Estate to build, after submitting three different sets of plans. Clause 14 of the 1895 deed provided that no dwelling houses were to be erected until the plans thereof had been submitted to and approved by the committee elected under the terms of the deed. The Prices sought a declaration from the court that the Committee's approval had been unreasonably withheld and that they were entitled to proceed without consent. The application was dismissed, it being held that there was no general principle of law that a contract requiring the consent of one party to be obtained by the other implies that such consent is not to be unreasonably withheld. The Committee was bound only to act honestly and in good faith and not for some improper purpose. Further, it was held that while it might be appropriate and would normally be convenient for the Committee to give reasons for its decisions, there was no legal duty on the Committee to do so. (The position was thus held to be comparable to that of the directors of a private company who refuse an application for the transfer of shares).[13] In the course of his judgment, Millett J. said:

> Thus for 90 years the stipulations in the deed of mutual covenant
> have formed a local law, democratically administered by a
> committee elected by a majority of the owners of land comprised

in the estate, the committee itself having an express power to act by a majority. It is conceded for the purpose of the present application that the present committee is the lawful committee established by the deed of mutual covenant and has the powers conferred on it by that deed. It must, I think, follow from that concession that the present plot owners who elect them are the mutual covenantors within the meaning of the deed and may exercise the powers conferred on them by that deed.

The covenants in question were restrictive but no argument was offered on the general question of the enforceability of such covenants against successors in title of original covenantees.

Enforceability of mutual covenants

On the issue of the enforceability of a scheme using a deed of mutual covenant a major clarification was at long last achieved, in a 1957 case already mentioned, *Halsall v. Brizell*. This case represented something of a triumph for the draftsmen of the 1840s, particularly as its ruling extends beyond mere enforcement of restrictions to the imposing and enforcing of positive obligations against persons not parties to the original deed. The case concerned Cressington Park in Liverpool, one of whose residents refused to pay the proportion of road maintenance charges deemed to be his due proportion by the then Committee. It could be said that the Committee brought about the dispute by trying to change the method of division of the charge. Instead of levying it in proportion to the size of the plot, 'a due and just proportion' as hitherto, the Committee decided that, where a house had been subdivided, it was fair to double the proportionate assessment on that plot.[14] The plaintiff succeeded to the extent that it was held that the original mode of assessment should continue, but on the principle of the enforceability of the positive obligation to pay for the maintenance, the Committee was successful. The maxim, 'He who takes the benefit must accept the burden of a deed', was brought into play. Because the roads, sewers and the promenade along the sea wall continued to be held by the trustees for the benefit of residents, the residents relied on the deed to give them 'easements of user' of these facilities, hence use of the facilities carried the obligation to pay towards their maintenance. On the facts of the case, there was clearly a close connection between the benefit and the burden. However, the principle having been revitalised with regard to deeds, it has subsequently been extended (by Lord Denning) to mere contracts.[15]

The success of the residents' committee in *Halsall v. Brizell* may have encouraged others to feel more optimistic about the prospects of success in litigating similar schemes. In 1965, in *Baxter v. Four Oaks Properties Limited*, a building scheme in Sutton Coldfield established by a deed of mutual covenant of 27 April 1891 was upheld, although damages were awarded in lieu of injunction.[16] In the course of his judgment, Cross J. said:

> With the passage of time it became apparent that there was no particular virtue in the execution of a deed of mutual covenant save as evidence of the intention of the parties – and what came to be called 'building schemes' were enforced by the courts if satisfied that it was the intention of the parties that the various purchasers should have rights inter se, even though no attempt was made to bring them into direct contractual relations.

Cross J. had earlier pointed out the difficulty which might arise where such a deed was signed over a number of years. For if one of the early purchasers was dead by the time a later purchaser signed the deed, it would be difficult, in attempting to enforce covenants against the later purchaser or his successors in title, to found the right of successors in title of the deceased earlier purchaser on any contract between the two original purchasers, even though each had signed the deed.

A further clarification arose because the plaintiffs in *Baxter v. Four Oaks Properties Limited* argued that since *Elliston v. Reacher* it was necessary for all building schemes to adhere strictly to the requirements laid down in that case. There had been no antecedent lotting of the whole of the Sutton Coldfield estate, but it was held that, while that may be a necessary part of the evidence of intention in cases where there is no deed of mutual covenant, the existence of such a deed can of itself be evidence of intention without other circumstantial evidence being necessary.

A footnote to the two previous cases is provided by *Four Oaks Properties Limited v. Hadley and Others*, a briefly reported Court of Appeal decision.[17] It was held that the non-profitmaking company managing the Four Oaks Estate could only require the defendants, the owners of 18,

Bracebridge Road, to make a contribution to the cost of maintaining and repairing the two roads which abutted their property. The original scheme had required the defendants to contribute on that basis, but since the 1920s costs had been apportioned equally among all 260 or so householders in proportion to their property frontage, without regard to where on the estate's thirteen roads repairs had been done. It was held that neither the defendants nor their predecessors in title had ever contracted to contribute on the new basis, nor had the covenant itself ever been modified; all that had happened was that the defendants' predecessors had chosen to make payments under the new system which they thought of benefit to them.

To succeed, the management company had to identify some benefit enjoyed by the defendants to which the burden of contributing to the global cost in some way attached. That benefit had to be the right to use the roads in respect of which the contribution was sought.

The management company was unable to identify the specific benefit required. There was no evidence of a right of way over the other estate roads and even if the defendants had a right to use the roads, there was no evidence that the right was granted conditionally by deed or contract requiring the defendants or their predecessors to contribute to the upkeep of the roads not adjoining their properties; nor could the management company establish an implied collateral contract made at the time the defendants bought their house. The decision is in line with *Halsall v. Brizell* – the original deed is enforceable but not later variations made without the consent of individual proprietors.

Building schemes by intention

The third method by which building schemes were created was simply as a matter of intention, the intent being evidenced by requirements defined later in *Elliston v. Reacher*. If a vendor sold lots subject to the same or similar covenants, the courts might find a scheme of development to exist, and this would enable a successor in title of an original purchaser to sue any other purchaser of a plot on the estate, without showing any express assignment of the benefit of the covenants to the former. Such a scheme was upheld in 1970 in *Re Dolphin's Conveyance*.[18] Robert Dolphin, a mid-Victorian solicitor, owned over 200 acres of land near Birmingham, which included both the Selly Hill Estate, the subject of this case, and the Selly Hall Estate, sold off by Dolphin in the early 1860s and held to be subject to a building scheme in an earlier apparently unreported decision of Swinfen Eady J. After the sale of the Selly Hall Estate, the remaining land passed to Dolphin's sisters on his death in December 1870. The sisters, and later a nephew, Watts, sold the 30 acres identified as the Selly Hill Estate in nine lots, subject to the same covenants, each purchaser covenanting with the sisters or with Watts, and the vendors also covenanting that 'they their heirs or assigns will procure a covenant from each purchaser or lessee upon Selly Hill Estate to the effect of those seven stipulations'. In his judgment, Stamp J. quoted the above from a conveyance and concluded as follows. 'As a matter of construction of the conveyances, I find that what was intended, as well by the vendors as the several purchasers, was to lay down what has been referred to as a local law for the estate for the common benefit of all the several purchasers of it.'

The judiciary and building schemes
After *Elliston v. Reacher* in 1908 (noted at the end of Chapter 3), where the scheme was upheld, it seems that the courts were in general reluctant to uphold building schemes, and few cases are reported on the subject until the 1950s. It is not possible to ascribe definite reasons for this, but certainly, the temper of the times was against restrictions on the use of land. After the 1914-1918 war successive governments made a great effort to increase the rate of house building and re-development in general, by means chiefly of subsidies.[19] Hence, when it was proposed to reform the law of property to produce a simplified and coherent set of rules, a provision to enable restrictive covenants to be modified or discharged was proposed and eventually became law, Section 90 of the Law of Property Bill of 1921 became Section 84 of the Law of Property Act of 1925. The property statutes were passed by the House of Lords three times before being accepted into the Government timetable and so passed by the House of Commons. In the course of a debate in the House of Lords in April 1921 regarding this particular section of the bill, Lord Phillimore said:

> As I understand the object of the clause, it is not dealing with the common case of restrictive covenants in a lease, but what the

Court of Chancery calls a building scheme ... It does or it may happen with the lapse of time, that these things become unreasonable and obsolete and that if anybody could be got to deal with them, they would be modified. The difficulty, of course, is that the land has got into a great many hands, that it may be mortgaged, that it may be settled, and that the practical difficulty of getting the concurrence of everybody is too great. I recognise that it is desirable that there should be some person or body, or authority, who should be able to dispense with these covenants in very exceptional cases, because after all it is very hard upon a gentleman who has bought a quiet little house to which to retire with his family on the faith and trust that it is what is called a residential neighbourhood, if he suddenly has a rookery put up next to him, or a public house, or the whole of the street is converted into a street of shops. Therefore, it ought to be done very gingerly and carefully.[20]

He proposed an amendment giving the power to the High Court, rather than to the Official Arbitrators appointed for the purpose of the Acquisition of Land (Assessment of Compensation) Act of 1919 (the Authority). But he stated - 'it was represented to me ... that the Judges themselves were not willing to have this duty cast on the Judges of the Chancery Division – but the friendly suggestion came to me that I should leave the Authority, but give an appeal to the High Court of Justice'. The latter amendment was passed.

In 1922, when the House of Commons was debating this section, Dalrymple White, the member for Southport, welcomed a further amendment which extended the clause to leaseholds. He said that many people noticed almost with dismay that the word 'freehold' had been inserted in the bill, therefore cutting 'leasehold' out of this clause, and he further noted that the amendment was only in favour of leases for 100 years or more. In his own constituency the vast majority of leases were for 99 years and that applied also to Liverpool and many other towns and cities. White proposed an amendment to 90 years, whereupon it was pointed out that this would not help those areas where the 75-year lease was usual. The eventual section applied to leases of 70 years or more. Another M.P. was sure that by the amendment not only would tenants be enormously benefitted, but the development of whole areas in the neighbourhood of towns would be greatly facilitated.[21] The general view was that Section 84 had done little more than give power to the Authority, later the Lands Tribunal, to discharge or modify restrictive covenants in circumstances where an injunction would in any case have been refused in court. The section is said by Jolly to have been based on the dictum of Lord Lindley in *Knight v. Simmonds* in 1896, to the effect that whatever the explanation of the altered state of things may be, if the object to be attained by a covenant cannot be attained, then equitable relief to enforce it must be refused.[22] Jolly considered that the section, which confers on officials wider and more flexible powers of giving relief than had ever before been exercised by the courts, and which did not confine those powers to the case of building schemes, was expressed, 'like most modern legislation', in loose and ambiguous language.[23]

It is conceivable that the reluctance of judges to find in favour of building schemes was in part the result of a general feeling that it was not in the national interest that old schemes should be enforced. However, by the 1960s, another phase of expansion of building had begun; town and country planning had proved not to answer all the problems of preserving the individual character of small areas and the courts returned to looking more kindly on Victorian schemes. The difficulties now passed to builders. In the 1960s and 1970s, builders wished to build on a larger scale than their Victorian counterparts generally did and were also often seeking to demolish old houses and to redevelop sites completely. Old covenants were inconvenient. As A'Court puts it: 'Potentially the worst situation for the developer is where the deed creating the covenant creates a building scheme … The practical problem … is to ascertain how many potential claimants there are.'[24] The usual solution is to insure, after attempting to find claimants by advertising, since the Lands Tribunal procedure is regarded as too cumbersome.

With the growth of interest in conservation and heritage issues, builders are now less likely to be allowed to demolish Victorian areas wholesale and are more commonly refurbishing the relevant property. Covenant problems are thus less likely to arise. However, the issue has shifted rather than totally disappeared; builders of the 1990s (and no doubt in the next century) are more likely to be developing greenfield sites, consequently their concern is the effect of the covenants they themselves create for the benefit of residents of new estates. The difficulty which they face — which equally faced their Victorian counterparts — is that if a building scheme is created on estates which they build, it may prevent them from developing in the most profitable way retained adjacent land. It had been common for a vendor to reserve a right to vary the lotting and covenants on land retained and it had been considered likely that such a provision might negative any intention to create a building scheme.[25] However, in *Elliston v. Reacher* Parker J. observed that if there were no scheme, the common vendor would not be bound and there would be no need to insert such a dispensing power. Such a power was then thought a marker of intention and thus to point towards a scheme. In Key and Elphinstone's 1914 *Precedents*, a precedent is offered which, on the decision in *Earl of Zetland v. Hislop*, negatives the creation of a scheme, which, if found, would be binding on the vendor as well as on the purchasers and would prevent development of the remaining part of the estate in a different manner from that represented to earlier purchasers.[26] Most recently such a power has been held to be of little effect in deciding whether or not a scheme was intended.[27] In Prideaux's 1913 *Precedents*, it was recommended that to prevent all question of what might have been intended, mutual deeds of covenant should be used. Alternatively, the conveyance to each purchaser should include, in addition to the covenants with the vendor, a declaration that he was entitled to the benefit of similar covenants entered into by the other purchaser, and that, as regards any plots not already sold, the same should be subject to the like restrictions.[28]

In other words, once *Elliston v. Reacher* had confirmed that intention was the basis of a scheme, it became necessary for vendors and, more recently, builders to decide from the outset whether or not a scheme is to be created. Any decision is better than none. For example, a building company developed an estate on an open plan, selling some plots freehold, although most leasehold. The 'open plan' was spoilt by incursions of sheep and horses and one of the freehold plot owners erected a fence in breach of covenant. The company sought an order in 1970 to compel him to remove the fence, but the defendant obtained a stay of action to permit an application to the Lands Tribunal under Section 84.[29] In 1971 the company applied to the Chancery Division for the removal of the stay on the grounds that the Lands

Tribunal did not have jurisdiction, since the covenant was binding only on the defendant personally and hence did not affect land, and that it was not in any event a restrictive covenant but one imposing a positive obligation.[30] Megarry J. held that the covenant was restrictive (though 'hybrid' in that parts of it were positive) and that it was eminently suitable for running with the land. Towards the end of his judgment, he said:

> At the hearing of the motion and cross-motion last year, the company was zealous for the enforcement of the 'open plan' on its estate, as being for the preservation of the amenities of all concerned. Zeal has now been displaced by aversion. The company is contending that the covenants entered into for this purpose are frail things that were never intended to bind successors in title but were intended to be personal to the first purchasers, dropping off as soon as any of them died or conveyed the land. No doubt the leasehold covenants would continue enforceable so long as the leases run; but amidst all the leaseholds there would be these freehold plots (seven in all) in respect of which the grand design was to be preserved only so long as the original purchasers continued the owners. Estate developers no doubt do bizarre things from time to time, but I have not previously encountered such an unexplained and apparently inexplicable eccentricity as in this case the company has now contended that it intended to exhibit ... I also find it a little surprising that nothing has been said about a scheme of development save that both counsel asserted that there was none; for the restrictions and parts of the evidence have features about them which point to a scheme ...

He concluded by observing sardonically that 'there may be deep waters in this case of which I know nothing'.

At present there are opposing views as to whether it is preferable to aim for a building scheme or not. One recent authority opines that –

> where there is a fairly comprehensive list of estate restrictions, then the obvious intention of the developer is that they are for the common good, and as no sane builder wishes to be involved in the administration, once he divests himself of all interest in it at the

end of the development, it is almost inconceivable that the developer in these circumstances does not intend to set up a building scheme, whether or not he says so in the transfers of the plots. We have therefore established that it is desirable to set up a building scheme.[31]
His precedent transfer form for such a scheme contains a clause giving wide powers to the vendor to vary the layout, etc., and also 'to withdraw, release, vary or abandon' any of the restrictions, covenants or relevant provisions. The author admits that he has found Chancery counsel horrified by the existence of such a clause, but he is unrepentant that its inclusion makes no difference following the Wembley Park case. An example of this mode of thinking appeared in the *Daily Telegraph* in 1987 in an article on Myrtle Gardens, a block of ex-council flats in Liverpool refurbished and sold on long leases by Barratt. The residents were given an automatic share in the running of the management committee, but only two of them had to date shown interest in taking responsibility, and out of 278 flats, only 20 residents attended the committee's annual general meeting. Barratt's manager was said to have declared – 'we are just the ground landlords now and we cannot go on running it for ever'.

A completely opposite view is, however, offered by A'Court. His precedent attempts to give the builder the best of all worlds. Covenants to be given by a purchaser are stated to benefit retained land and every part of it, the retained land being defined as the remainder of land comprised within the registered title to the estate and any adjoining land which the vendor might own within 80 years from the date of the transfer (although he admits that this extension to later-acquired property may not be valid). Another clause reserves to the vendor the right to waive or release any of the covenants, etc., and states that the purchaser's covenants shall not impose any restrictions on the vendor, nor be deemed to create a building scheme. As there is no express assignment of the benefit of any covenants to a purchaser, the author believes that a plaintiff purchaser would have to prove that the benefit had technically been attached to the plot in question.[32] This approach seems to have been favoured by, for example, the developers of the Tadworth Park Estate in Surrey.[33] This is clearly intended to be a superior residential development to be sold freehold, with some of the houses having secure, gated access roads, and overall access to 'amenity land'.[34] Clause 3 of the standard form of transfer states that – 'Neither the development of the Estate nor this deed creates a building scheme'. The amenity of the estate is instead to be protected by requiring purchasers to become shareholders in Tadworth Park Woodlands Limited in respect of the amenity land, and, additionally, in the case of houses having gated access, Lancaster Mews (Tadworth Park) Limited. The covenants themselves, specifically stated to be for the benefit of the company, are modest; no additional building for five years without the company's consent, save for garden sheds and greenhouses; no trade or business inconsistent with the use of the property as a dwelling; no animals except normal domestic pets; no damage to trees or plants and an obligation on a purchaser to maintain fences and to keep grassed the unenclosed parts of the garden. No doubt the more expensive the house, the fewer covenants are deemed necessary.

In conclusion, it appears that nowadays, when the builder has made the initial decision as to density of occupation and type of building, the residents themselves have little influence on the nature of an estate. But in the early-Victorian estates to be described in the following chapters, the covenants had to start from the 'greenfield' point of density, value and style of building, as well as of use thereafter; consequently, more covenants were imposed and residents carried the whole burden of development themselves.

NOTES TO CHAPTER 4

1. Maurice Spiers, *Victoria Park, Manchester* (Manchester, 1976), 4. Spiers mentions, as a socially comparable development, Cressington Park in Liverpool.

2. 7 Will 4 c.30.

3. A similar tontine scheme was used for the development of Princes Park in Liverpool, as shown below.

4. Ironically, this was none other than Sir William Reynold Anson, Warden of All Souls College, Oxford and author of *The Principles of the English Law of Contract* and *The Law and Custom of the Constitution*, who 'combined real learning with a wide knowledge of affairs' (*DNB*).

5. Spiers, *Victoria Park*, 42.

6. (1843) 2 Hare 461; 67 ER 189.

7. J.G. Cooper and A.D. Power, *A history of West Derby* (Liverpool, 1982), 219.

8. (1970) 23 P & CR 102. The amendment was by S.28 of the Law of Property Act of 1969.

9. W.A.Jolly, *Restrictive covenants affecting land* (London 1909), 49.

10. 7 & 8 Victoria, c.76.

11. (1986) 53 P & CR 257.

12. According to the title deeds and a supplemental deed of 2 February 1896.

13. *Re Smith & Fawcett Ltd.*, [1942] Ch. 304.

14. The reference to 'a due and just proportion' is in the Deed of Covenant of 19 August 1851.

15. *E.R.Ives Investment Ltd. v. High* [1967] 2 QB 379.

16. [1965] Ch 816.

17. (1986) 83 L. S. Gaz. 2326 CA.

18. [1970] 1 Ch 654 (sub nom. *Birmingham Corporation v. Boden and others*)

19. For instance, by the Housing Act of 1919. The high standard of local authority housing that was aimed at proved too expensive and government financing was discontinued in 1921. In 1923 the Conservative government announced a new initiative designed to stimulate private building; in 1924 the first Labour government introduced a new Housing Act, building on the 1919 basis. See M. Swennarton, *Homes fit for heroes* (London, 1981).

20.   *Hansard, Lords* 44: 996.

21.   *Hansard, Commons* 155: 433-4.

22.   [1896] 1 Ch 653.

23.   Jolly, *Restrictive covenants*, 2nd ed. (London, 1931), 117.

24.   P.M. A'Court, *Estate conveyancing* (London, 1984), 67.

25.   *Osborne v. Bradley* [1903] 2 Ch 446 at 455.

26.   H.W. Elphinstone and F.T. Maw, eds, *Key and Elphinstone's Precedents in conveyancing*, 10th ed. (2 vols, London, 1914), 1: 378, referring to (1882) 7 App.Cas. 427 at 452.

27.   *Re Wembley Park Estate Company's Transfer [1968] Ch 491.*

28.   B.L. Cherry and R. Beddington, eds, *Prideaux's Precedents in conveyancing*, 21st ed., 2 vols (London 1913), 2: 120.

29.   *Shepherd Homes Ltd. v. Sandham* [1971] Ch 340.

30.   *Shepherd Homes Ltd. v. Sandham (No.2)* [1971] 2 All ER 1267.

31.   J. Cawthorne, *Residential estate conveyancing practice and precedents* (London, 1983), 143.

32.   A'Court. *Estate conveyancing*, 137.

33.   Conveyancing documentation seen by courtesy of John Mowlem Homes Ltd.

34.   According to the sales brochure (John Mowlem Homes Ltd) - 'a vast expanse of open park land studded with majestic mature trees'.

LIVERPOOL ESTATES

5: Liverpool Park Estates: (1) Fulwood Park

A large area to the east of the ancient borough of Liverpool became the home in the nineteenth century of three of Liverpool's park estates. As a borough, Liverpool is generally dated from the grant of King John's charter in 1208, the king supposedly having noted the convenience of the harbour for use as a base for his Irish campaigns. The same king acquired as a royal hunting ground the deer park of Toxteth, lying to the east of the borough, which was then extended to cover about 2,300 acres and surrounded by a wall seven miles long.[1] The whole area was thereafter known as Toxteth Park. Seven centuries after these events the port of Liverpool had developed from a mere harbour for Ireland into a major Atlantic port. By the early nineteenth century its population was approaching 100,000, the greater part being crowded into 'streets long, narrow, crooked and dirty'.[2] But on rising ground away from the river wealthy merchants began to live in newly-formed streets, such as St Anne Street and Rodney Street, and some moved even further away from the port, its bustling docks and associated housing. As early as 1773 it was noted that -

> EVERTON, WAVERTREE and TOXTETH PARK are pleasant villages, which have of late years been much improved with country houses, which several of the principal inhabitants of Leverpool have built for their summer retreat.[3]

The rapid population growth of Liverpool in the later eighteenth century led Charles William Molyneux, first earl of Sefton, to embark on a scheme to improve his property and his income, by commencing a new town on his estate, which included a large part of Toxteth Park.

The Seftons and residential development

Toxteth Park, when granted by the crown to the the the Stanleys, earls of Derby, was disparked in the 1590s.[4] By the early seventeenth century the park was farmed by tenants: its surrounding wall survived, wholly or partly, for most of the century.[5] Around 1610 the freehold of the park passed from the Stanleys to the Molyneux for a purchase price of £1,000.[6] For long Toxteth Park continued to preserve an exclusively rural character. But in 1771, 52 acres of farmland adjoining the boundary of the borough of Liverpool, on the south side of Parliament Street, were laid out for building, and in 1775 Lord

Sefton obtained an Act of Parliament enabling him to grant building leases.[7] An enterprising builder, one Cuthbert Bisbrown, took the most active part in the creation of the new town, which was to be called Harrington (after Lord Sefton's wife, Isabella, daughter of the second earl of Harrington). The land was let on building leases which proved not to have been well drafted. A late-Victorian local historian claimed that -

> In laying out the land a grave error was committed, the results of which have been very serious, and will operate injuriously for ages to come. The leading lines of street were laid out judiciously enough at right angles, and of ample width; but the interior of the blocks so divided was left to be arranged as chance or cupidity might direct. Hence arose sub-divisions of mean narrow streets, filled with close, gloomy courts, into which as many dwellings as possible were packed, irrespective of light and air. The result has been the impression of an inferior character on this quarter of the town, which it has never been able to recover.[8]

Because of this early attempt by the Sefton estate office to respond to the demand for land in the market, the north-western part of the Park came to have a radically different character from the southern end of the Park, where instead, in time, the better-off came to live in its continuing semi-rural environment.[9]

The spending of the Seftons exceeded their income. In 1777, the earl sold his reversionary right in the manor and lordship of Liverpool to the Corporation, for £2,500.[10] Despite efforts to improve the income of the family estates, by 1791 debts of some £40,000 had accumulated. A lengthy memorandum written by the earl's steward, John Webster, offered advice on ways of clearing this debt over a period of sixteen years. The agent pointed out that many of the remaining agricultural lettings in Toxteth Park were lettings for lives where the last 'life' was now of an advanced age; if these lettings fell in at a reasonable rate and the property were re-let for a term of years at current market rents, then the income would accordingly rise. This plan adopted throughout the earl's estate, coupled with a strict regime of economy, would avoid the need to sell land with the 'degrading and indignity ... in the eyes and minds of the public' which such sales entailed.[11] In 1795, immediately after the first earl's death, Webster urged on the new earl the advice previously tendered to his father: that land should be let at rack rents as lives dropped so that the debts could be paid off without any loss to creditors, social face could be saved, and land need not be sold.[12] But the second earl and his new wife were not prepared to live on a mere £3,065 per annum, whatever the prospect of an increase in the future when the debts had been paid off, and hence did not hesitate to sell land. It appears that in 1798 no fewer than 225 lots of property were put up for sale.[13] Again, in July 1812 auction particulars were prepared of 'sundry parcels of freehold land situate in Toxteth Park, contiguous to the town of Liverpool'.[14] Sale of land at the other end of the park had already taken place, as we shall see. The Seftons were clearly meeting a local demand for land for development, in the circumstances now to be described.

The suburbanization of Liverpool
In 1832 the Report of the Parliamentary Boundary Commissioners summarised the recent history of Liverpool, and in particular what we may call its 'suburbanization', as follows.

The Borough and Parish of Liverpool are co-extensive. The town however, reaches far beyond the boundaries of the Borough on every side. ... The great extension and rapid increase in building and the probability that building will long continue to increase, have induced us to propose what may at first sight be considered an extended boundary. From the best information which we have been able to procure, we find the increase of Houses in the circuit of the adjoining Townships may be taken at seven hundred per annum. The main cause of the extension of the town is the rapid increase of its trade, the consequent construction of the new Docks, the progressive addition to the population and the constant and rapidly increasing communication by steam with Ireland and the intercourse with Manchester and the other surrounding towns by the Rail-roads and Canals. ... The increase of luxury appears to have followed the increase of wealth; the persons formerly living in small houses in the densely peopled parts of the Town have been induced to seek more commodious habitations in the suburbs; this change may be considered as now in full operation.

... At present, the price of land for building is very high, both in the Town and on the outskirts. As much as 10 guineas a sq. yd. has been given in the middle of the town; and the price of building ground in the different directions immediately surrounding the Town is from 5/- to 15/- the sq. yd. or from £1,000 to £3,000 per acre. Even as far as four miles from Liverpool in very favourable situations £500 per statute acre is not, we are told, an infrequent price.[15]

The boundary extension proposed by the commissioners included that part of Toxteth Park which adjoined the borough and which had been built up. The 1821 census had recorded the population of Toxteth Park as totalling 24,067 (out of a town population of 165,221), making it by far the largest of the townships adjoining the borough.

Accordingly, the Municipal Corporations Act of 1835 extended the borough boundaries to coincide with the parliamentary boundaries fixed in 1832. The 1835 act initiated great changes in the administration of the borough. Prior to the act, the Council had consisted of a corporation of forty citizens, 'all of them men of excellent standing in the town'.[16] Although a self-perpetuating oligarchy, and in the spirit of the times one with the limited view that what was good for themselves and for the freemen of the borough was adequate municipal administration, nevertheless in the later-eighteenth and early-nineteenth centuries the Council displayed considerable entrepreneurial qualities in developing the docks and acting as trustee of the consequent Dock Estate; some part of the profits of this enterprise no doubt trickled down.[17] The Council had also introduced occasional Improvement Acts; for instance, an act of 1785 had resulted in the widening of three main streets, Castle Street, Dale Street and Water Street.[18] But the Council did not take any steps to gain overall control of the way the town centre was developing; on being memorialised by a group of leading townsmen who suggested a 'spacious, handsome public road' round the old township, the council simply replied that this could not be entertained.[19] The consequence of such a hands-off attitude was that Liverpool took too few steps to meet the challenge of very rapid population growth. By the early nineteenth century the original town centre was in large part a crowded, unhealthy, insecure locality. As the merchants moved out, their houses were taken over by the poor; even the cellars of houses and warehouses were turned into dwellings. In 1790, a survey of the town showed that there were 8,148 inhabited houses, with 1,728 inhabited cellars the homes of 6,780 individuals, more than one-ninth of the inhabitants of the town.[20] With little effort by the magistrates to limit the number of licensed premises, it was calculated in 1795 that one in seven houses was licensed for the sale of liquor.[21] Until a re-organisation in 1811, there was no police force during the day, and only a few old and feeble watchmen at night.[22]

In this period, Toxteth Park, Everton and the other areas fringing the borough were even less provided for administratively. Being outside Corporation concern, these districts had to rely on manorial jurisdiction and the county justices. The Report which preceded the Municipal Corporations Act of 1835 included evidence which alleged that Toxteth, in particular, was noted as the resort of the most lawless and disorderly classes.[23] The wealthier residents of the southern part of the park paid a few guineas a year to maintain a patrol, but without much effect.[24] At the north end of Toxteth Park - Harrington as it had been intended to be named - the streets were unsafe and the area was described as 'The Alsatia of Liverpool'.[25]

As is well known, overcrowding, lack of sanitation and inadequate water supply led to a great deal of disease in early nineteenth-century Liverpool. Even before the massive Irish immigration of 1846-1847 the Registrar-General had reported in 1844 that Liverpool's mortality statistics were 'extremely unfavourable'.[26] Between 1838 and 1845 inclusive, 14,982 houses were built in Liverpool, partly as the result of a local law forbidding the use of cellars as dwelling places, but events overwhelmed attempts to improve the residential condition of the poor of the town.[27] The 'reformed' municipal authorities grappled with these problems, spending large sums on sewerage, cleansing, bath- and wash-houses, housing, and improvements to the water supply. Turning to private amenities, gas became available for street-lighting, and in 1841 the Liverpool Gaslight Company obtained statutory power to extend its undertaking to Toxteth Park, Wavertree, Everton and other outer areas.[28] But in general conditions improved only slowly. In consequence of these unfavourable circumstances within the original borough area during the early decades of the century, the better-off experienced an ever-increasing incentive to move to the suburbs.

Other factors encouraged the move. The increased expenditure of the
Council after the 1834 reform had to be met locally, the dock and other older
revenues proved to be insufficient, and higher rates had to be levied. It may
therefore have been a consequence of the Municipal Corporations Act that all
the developments around Liverpool discussed below occurred outside the
extended boundary of the borough. Not until 1895 was the rest of Toxteth
Park, with Wavertree, Walton and more of West Derby, placed within a new
Liverpool boundary. A further factor may have been the availability of
freehold land. As noted in Chapter 1, the Corporation owned more than half
of the area of the original borough and it was from 1820 the practice to lease
this land for terms of 75 years, renewable on each transfer on payment of a
fine. Evidence given to the 1886 Select Committee on Town Holdings shows
that both the Sefton and Derby estate offices had also adopted this system,
as had 'Harrington' after the Toxteth Park Estate Act of 1775.[29] In general,
therefore, freehold land was only available from small landowners, these
being less likely to opt for long-term gain from future leasehold renewals
than was the case with the impersonal Corporation and the estates offices of
aristocratic landlords. To make any substantial capital sum out of releasing
land for building, a small landowner had to sell the freehold, the premium
or fine obtained for a lease being relatively trifling.

In evidence about the Sefton estate presented to the 1889 Select
Committee on Town Holdings, it was stated that it had been the practice
formerly to make sales in fee simple; that both systems had existed side by
side but that the late John Stewart, agent for Lord Sefton, had decided not to
sell the freehold on the estate because it was more profitable to lease and
grant continual renewals on a scale assessed on the improved value of the
land.[30] John Stewart clearly had more of a free hand than his predecessor
had had in the 1790s, who had argued in the same way but been over-ruled
by the second earl. This, as we have seen, had allowed freehold land to
become available in Toxteth Park, and by the 1840s the southern part was
becoming an attractive place to live.[31] The move to the suburbs, in this case
to Toxteth Park, provided the opportunity for the formation of park estates.

A prefatory venture: Princes Park
Information on the history of Princes Park is very limited and unlike the later park estates it has not survived in anything like its initial form: discussion will therefore be brief. Around 1840 Richard Vaughan Yates purchased 44 acres of ground inside the municipal boundary but as yet unbuilt upon, being on the outskirts of the town. His plan was to form a park, the central portion of which was to be open to the public, the project to be financed from the rents of substantial houses to be built round the periphery. Yates paid £50,000 for the land; it was said that his total outlay on the project was about £70,000. Unfortunately, the returns during his lifetime were not good, 'the times not being propitious'.[32] As stated earlier, Princes Park was laid out in 1842 by Joseph Paxton, his earliest effort at public park planning.[33] The first houses around the park were built on the east side by a company formed on the principle of a tontine. Advertisements making calls of £25 on shareholders in the Princes Park Tontine were placed at intervals in the local press.[34] St Paul's church, now demolished, was built in 1848. Coincidentally or otherwise, its first incumbent, Dr Hugh McNeile, forms a link with Fulwood Park, where he was one of the earliest residents.

Fulwood Park established
That part of the township of Toxteth Park remaining outside the borough being still of a predominantly rural character it was not regarded as appropriate to include it in the parliamentary boundary in 1832, or in the town boundary in 1835. Contemporary maps show a few substantial houses in extensive grounds, most of which are now recalled only by the names of the roads running through these grounds, along which smaller houses have since been built. Along Aigburth Road, running down towards Aigburth Vale from the 1835 boundary, were several of these houses, whose details give something of the flavour of the burgeoning residential area. On the north side of Aigburth Road was 'Parkfield', owned by a Mr Tayleur, but beyond land also named as his were fields still belonging to Lord Sefton. On the south side of the road were 'Laurel Mount' and 'Grove House' owned by a Mr Dempsey, and also land owned by John Cragg, owner of the Mersey Iron Foundry in Tithebarn Street. This ironmaster, together with Thomas Rickman, built the 'cast iron' church of St. George at Everton, but Cragg

also built the church of St Michael's in the Hamlet, near to his own house in Toxteth Park, 'Hollybank'. Nearby, Cragg and Rickman built five other houses with Gothick names: 'The Cloister', 'The Friars', 'The Nunnery', 'The Friary', and 'The Hermitage'. Continuing down Aigburth Road, a Miss Backhouse owned 'Old Hall'; W. Woodhouse, 'Ivy Cottage'; William Peatt Bushby, 'Larkfield', and William Smith, 'Fulwood Lodge', later called 'Fulwood [or Fullwood] House'.[35] Smith, who before moving to Toxteth Park had lived on St Anne Street in its early fashionable days, in 1839, in association with his brother Alexander, purchased the land to the east of his house, the object of the purchase being the division of the land into lots for sale on strict terms which would ensure that the right type of neighbour moved there.[36]

In the Sefton papers at Preston is a licence dated 9 December 1803 which deals, *inter alia*, with the land that became Fulwood Park. The licence from the earl of Sefton permitted a farmer to sell to a Liverpool butcher the leases of the 14-acre White House farm and nine acres of adjoining fields.[37] In 1808 the butcher obtained from the earl the freehold of the land. In 1840 William and Alexander Smith, by then then owners of the fields, drew up Articles of Agreement which contained restrictive clauses and which were afterwards signed by various purchasers of the different allotments. For instance, none of the houses erected on this land was to cost less than £1,500 and each was to be built of stone, or brick, cemented or stuccoed, and not higher than two storeys.[38] The contract for the purchase of the land was entered into with the executors of the former owner, William Bunnell, by William Smith and Alexander Smith the younger, both of Liverpool, merchants.

William Smith of Fulwood Lodge appears in trade directories of Liverpool from as early as 1818, his business address being William Smith & Son, Merchants, 6 Exchange Buildings.[39] The 1841 census recorded him as living at Fullwood (sic) Lodge, aged 70, with his wife, Mary, aged 55, three daughters, and four children aged from five to eight all surnamed Smith, relationship unspecified. The family were looked after by one male and four female servants, and by Margaret Bernard, possibly a governess, while a coachman living at Fullwood Cottage most likely also belonged to the establishment. In 1847 the Tithe Map of this area recorded Fulwood Lodge as being in the possession of William Jones and William Smith was no longer recorded in the directories - presumably he had died.[40] The firm of William Smith and Son continued in the hands of Alexander Smith jnr., whose first traced appearance in the directories was in 1824 when he was living at Dingle Lodge, Toxteth Park (his address in the park thereafter frequently changed).[41] In a directory of 1841 he was described as a merchant and manufacturing chemist at 23, Seel Street, with an interest in indigo mills; by 1845, he had added insurance broking to his interests, and in 1847 he was also described as a money-broker; his last personal entry was in 1851, his address now 3, South Hill, Toxteth Park.[42] The firm of William Smith and Son continued to be listed at 6, Exchange Buildings, now in connection with William Digby Smith also of 3, South Hill.[43] The picture indicated by this evidence is that of a family in a long-established and successful way of business, the younger generation of which developed diversified business interests.

It is unclear, however, whether there was any substantial profit motive behind the development of Fulwood Park. In the recitals to a deed of release dated 23 July 1845 which conveyed a plot in Fulwood Park to the Reverend Hugh McNeile, it is stated that the two Smiths had agreed to purchase the land from the previous owner's executors for £13,900; but that no conveyance had yet been executed. Hence the conveyance of the land to McNeile was by direction of the Smiths in consideration of £755 10s paid to the executors in part payment of the purchase money due but in full payment for the plot conveyed.[44] This curious arrangement, which resulted in the vendors having to wait a considerable time for their money, was common in the case of all three of the Liverpool parks here studied. Nowhere in the available documents is the area purchased by the Smiths stated but measurement from the plan indicates that it was about 36 acres in all.[45] If the statement in 1832 by the Boundary Commissioners that land in a very favourable situation even four miles from Liverpool could sell for £500 per acre was correct, a price of £13,900 paid in the 1840s was modest, representing only about £390 per acre. The measurements given in the conveyance to McNeile indicate that he purchased a plot of about 6,682 square yards (1.4 acres) for £755 10s, a price nearer to £550 per acre. The Articles of Agreement required the Smiths to make a road from Aigburth

Road to the river, a good 1,000 yards distant, and for about 700 yards of its length it was to have footpaths as well, and they were also to erect a gate at the park entrance on Aigburth Road. The road area, which was to remain in the ownership of the trustees (its value presumably being divided among the lots), reduced the 36 acres available for plots. If all plots were priced like McNeile's, their total sale would have produced little over £15,000. It would therefore seem unlikely that any profit on the sale of the land can have been a significant one, although this does not of course rule out the possibility that the original intention had been otherwise.

The tithe map of 1847 shows that all the land had been transferred from the previous owner's executors to men who had signed the articles of agreement. The owners recorded as taking plots to the left of the entrance were William Henry Goore (five lots approximately); John Eden (one lot); William John Tomlinson (three lots); Charles Cotesworth (one lot); and Hugh McNeile (two lots). Samuel and James Holme took all the remainder of the land on that side down to the river (approximately eight acres); the Holmes were builders who put up six houses on the land. On the right side, John Holt had a stretch of land down to the river corresponding to that of the Holmes, plus one lot; John Yate Lee had two lots; Thomas Avison one lot; Robert Wynne one lot, and James Birkett had the remaining three lots, named as the 'Three Sixes'.[46] These lots as shown in 1847 correspond approximately to the original plan and intention. The land had thus been divided among eleven owners. The original plan had divided the entrance end of the land into 21 numbered lots while the Articles of Agreement referred to plots numbered to 30. Allowing for roads, this latter figure would accord with the purchase of an estimated 36 acres. All the individuals named above signed and sealed the articles of agreement except John Holt. Holt is not recorded in any census return as having lived in Fulwood Park although five houses were built on his land.[47]

Fulwood Park in operation

The 1840 articles of agreement are in fact a deed containing covenants made between the two Smiths of the first part; the several other persons who sign and seal it, that is, the plot purchasers, of the second part; and Charles Stewart Parker, merchant and Thomas Forsyth, broker of the third part, who are the trustees of the deed.[48] The road, footpaths and sewers were to be completed to the trustees' satisfaction; they were made responsible for the collection of sums due for the maintenance of the roads and sewers; if a contribution was not paid, then it was to be due to them as if it were a rent reserved by them as owners of the plot in question. A general meeting of the owners was to be held on the first Tuesday in January every year, at which meeting the maintenance contributions were to be decided. The meeting was empowered to appoint a committee to whom powers might be delegated, and a treasurer from among the owners for the time being, to act as the agent of the trustees in the collection of money. The onerous nature of the job of the trustees was therefore mainly a matter of appearance, although (as will be seen later) should legal action become necessary, then it had to be taken by the trustees and this could involve them in a certain amount of trouble. The trustees, Parker and Forsyth, do not appear to have had any connection with the scheme beyond their overseeing role. C.S. Parker appeared regularly in the directories as a member of the firm of T. Sandbach and Co., and he lived in and around Aigburth, in the vicinity of the park, from 1834 to at least 1862.[49] Thomas Forsyth appeared from 1827 to 1853 as a stock and share broker and in 1839 as an insurance broker, at various home addresses in the best town streets, St Anne Street, Canning Street, and Huskisson Street.[50] These men were presumably business acquaintances of the Smiths, perhaps members of the same clubs, who would, when called on, do a public-spirited favour. Subsequent trustees were to be elected by a general meeting of the proprietors. The deed was signed and sealed by the parties and purchasers indicated above, but it was also signed by Joseph Miller, J.P. Younghusband, George B. Carter, William Bower and T.B. Forwood. These men do not appear anywhere else in connection with the park.[51]

The covenants show that Fulwood Park was intended to be a very high-class residential locality. A density of only one house per acre was, and is, very low. (The permitted density in the other parks was approximately four houses to the acre.) In fact, since some purchasers took larger plots (formed of two or more lots), the density was even lower, and this has permitted some infill building in more recent times without breaking the covenants. The minimum sum to be expended on each house, outbuildings, fencing and gardens was to be £1,500. This again is a high figure: although it is difficult to estimate the present-day equivalent, the re-building cost for insurance purposes today would be probably £300,000 to £400,000. Between 1815 and 1850, the vast majority of houses built throughout Britain cost less than £1,000 and few exceeded £300. For £1,550, one could build a 'suitably ornate villa, with ground floor accommodation of a 388 sq. ft. drawing room, 352 sq. ft. dining room, breakfast room, kitchen, scullery, vestibule, cellars, larder, china pantry, coal store, two WCs, yard, stable and gig house'.[52]

The minimum required expenditure was probably easily exceeded by most of the original purchasers of multiple lots in Fulwood Park. When Thomas Avison, one of the earliest residents, decided to leave Liverpool for the South of England, his house was put up for auction on 2 February 1878; it was described in the auction particulars as a 'handsome and capitally-built residence, standing within its own grounds situate in Fulwood Park, near Liverpool'. This 'most excellent freehold house' had 'Kitchen and Flower Gardens, Two Conservatories, Vineries and Hot-houses, Plant-houses, Gardener's Cottage, Coachman's House, Excellent Stable, Harness Room, Coach-house, Piggeries, Poultry Enclosure, etc.'. The house was built by Messrs. Samuel and James Holme, 'which fact is in itself a guarantee of the capital finish and workmanship, in every particular, of the building.' The house stood on a single plot of the park stated to measure 10,710 sqare yards. A pencil note on the particulars records bidding between W.R. and W.; it started at £4,000, but after a final bid of £4,700 from W.R., the property was withdrawn. Reference is made in the Conditions of Sale to the covenants and conditions of the deed of 27 October 1840, a copy of which could be seen at the office of Avison and Morton, 18 Cook Street, or at the sale itself.[53]

As noted earlier, the covenants required all houses to be built of brick or stone, stuccoed or roughcast, and not higher than two storeys, exclusive of cellars and attics. The attics were to be lighted from the roof. These last two provisions were clearly to preserve the privacy of the residents by preventing overlooking, although when trees had grown it would in any case have been scarcely possible to see one house from another. Naturally, use of the buildings was limited to use as a dwelling house only, and not as a lodging-house or boarding-school, without the consent in writing of the majority of the other owners. Front boundary walls and railings on top of them were to be of uniform height and no close boarding was to be used to prevent persons from seeing through any railings or fence (an instance of assertive 'appropriation').[54] A guide recently produced by the Liverpool Heritage Bureau describes the style of the Fulwood Park houses as generally 'Italianate', and possibly there was informal pressure to conform to this style. The guide considers that the similarity in the detail on many of the 'villas' indicates that the same architect was responsible for these houses.[55]

It is impossible to say at this distance of time whose idea the scheme was; the various parties were, however, connected by place and business. William Smith, Charles Stewart Parker and Thomas Forsyth were members of the Liverpool Athenaeum in the 1830s, as were, from among the signatories of the articles of agreement, Avison, Eden, both Holmes, Birkett, Carter and Cotesworth.[56] Thomas and William Birkett, merchants of Liverpool, were named as trustees in the will of William Bunnel, gentleman: James Birkett, solicitor, was probably related to them, and William Smith, merchant, lived next door to him. The articles of agreement were probably drafted by the well-established firm of solicitors, Laces.[57] The witnesses to the signatures were mostly from Laces. Ambrose Lace witnessed two signatures, and other witnesses, Rigge, Myers and Edward Henry Roscoe, are shown in the Law Lists in 1840 and succeeding years as members of the firm. It is noted on the deed that Laces held the document from 1923 to 1960, so that the connection of the firm with Fulwood Park in a legal capacity continued.[58]

Turning to the early residents of Fulwood Park, Thomas Avison's house was built and occupied by 1847; an attorney and town councillor, Avison was president of the Law Library Society in 1844.[59] John Yate Lee, also resident by 1847, was a barrister and the Registrar of the Bankruptcy Court.[60] Hugh McNeile, who was referred to above, although a clergyman lived in considerable style. He and his wife seem to have been away from home on the night of the 1851 census. The head of the household for the occasion was therefore Elizabeth McNeile, clergyman's daughter, in charge of her two sisters and five brothers, ages ranging from 23 to 4, and also six resident servants, including a governess and a butler.[61] According to the census, the six proprietary families living in the park had between them 24 children under sixteen and 32 servants, and the servants had another eight children. With sundry nieces and visitors, there were in the park on the night of the 1851 census 84 individuals, almost all dependent on the earning capacity of five heads of household.[62] This is indeed a world which we now can scarcely appreciate. These wealthy, respectable, professional men may have been withdrawing from the crowded and insanitary centre of town but they were not aiming for a solitary life in the country - in Fulwood Park they were not going to be lonely or bereft of company. Yet of all these individuals, only twelve were adult males; one can see why Victorian men invented the gentlemen's club and were concerned to keep women out of it. The figures also show that the six women running these households had each a large staff: did they find time hang heavy on their hands?

Fulwood Park was not planned to be a large development. No more than 30 houses at the most seem to have been anticipated. In the event, because some purchasers took larger plots, fewer than that number were built. In 1851, there were six major houses occupied and five uninhabited. By the census of 1861, 13 houses were occupied. By 1871, 18 houses were occupied, one was empty and no further building seems to have taken place between then and the 1891 census. The new residents almost always described themselves as merchants, sometimes adding detail; they included Brazil merchants, East India merchants, ship-brokers, cotton-brokers, an iron-founder, a wholesale grocer, and the Prussian consul. The lawyers, so much involved in setting up the scheme, do not seem to have added to their earlier number in the park.

Today, most of the houses, old and new, remain as private residences, and such infill building as has taken place has only been with the consent of the trustees. Inevitably, departure from the style of building has been permitted - and the sum required to be spent has ceased to be difficult to comply with - but the principle of covenanted amenity has been maintained. Annual meetings of the residents are still held, at which the rate for the maintenance of the road is set and new trustees are elected when necessary. It is only in recent years that it has been felt advisable to confirm by deed the appointment of the trustees by the meeting.

As will be shown, the pattern of this scheme was copied for Grassendale Park and Cressington Park. Judicious permitting of departure from the covenants avoided major litigation over the years but when this did occur, in 1957, in relation to Cressington Park, the scheme was found to be effective, in that the positive covenants to maintain roads and other common amenities were found enforceable.[63] With the current popularity of conservation and the revival of interest in Victorian villas, it seems likely that, should a major breach of the covenants be proposed today, a challenge under Section 84 of the Law of Property Act as amended would not succeed. Furthermore, the revival of the economic fortunes of Liverpool is being felt in the housing market: large houses in an attractive position near to the newly re-claimed and landscaped river bank are again in demand. After passing through a phase of neglect between the wars, and some compromises since, Fulwood Park, as an amenity-led estate more or less fulfilling the original intentions of its founders, now seems to have a secure future.

NOTES TO CHAPTER 5

1.   Ramsay Muir, *A history of Liverpool* (Liverpool, 1907), 15. The park was originally fenced by Roger of Poitou, to whom William I granted the Honour of Lancashire, comprising all the land between the Ribble and the Mersey.

2.   According to Samuel Curwen in 1780: Muir, *History of Liverpool*, 270.

3.   W. Enfield, *An essay towards the history of Liverpool* (Warrington, 1773), 114.

4.   J.A. Picton, *Memorials of Liverpool* (2 vols, Liverpool, 1875), 2: 459.

5.   Muir, *History of Liverpool*, 112; Picton, *Memorials*, 458.

6.   There are varying accounts of this transaction: Thomas Baines, *History of the commerce and town of Liverpool* (Liverpool, 1852), 291; Picton, *Memorials*, 126; J. Stonehouse, *The streets of Liverpool* (Liverpool, 1870), 170; R. Griffiths, *The history of the royal and ancient park of Toxteth* (Liverpool, 1907); J. Touzeau, *The rise and progress of Liverpool 1550-1835* (Liverpool, 1910), 126; L. Hall, 'Toxteth Park Chapel in the seventeenth century', *Transactions of the Unitarian Historical Society*, 1933, 7.

7.   Parliament Street got its name at the time of the passing of this Act. The old boundary of Toxteth Park ran up Parliament Street to meet Smithdown Road, behind and beyond the Brook House (now a public house), and then down to the river at Jericho Lane: Muir, *History of Liverpool*, 15.

8.   Picton, *Memorials*, 460. Cf. 'a dense mass of mean streets, planned by Lord Sefton in 1775, as a means of obtaining a share in the prosperity of the thriving town, but not in any way under the control or oversight of the borough authorities': Muir, *History of Liverpool*, 243. Note that Liverpool was a 'town' until it became a 'city' in 1880.

9.   P. Booth, 'The background: people and the place', in Q. Hughes, ed., *Sefton Park* (Liverpool, 1984), 38.

10.   Muir, *History of Liverpool*, 145. In 1672 Lord Molyneux had leased the rights to the Corporation for 1,000 years. Charles William 'conformed to the established Church' in 1768 (the Molyneux having been previously Catholic) and was created Earl of Sefton in the Peerage of Ireland on 30 November 1771.

11.   Lancashire County Record Office: Sefton MSS, DDM 11/63. Another solution suggested was equally conventional - to make sure that the heir, Lord Molyneux, married well, say, to the daughter of a banker worth at least £60,000 a year.

12.   Ibid., DDM 11/69/22. A major drain on the earl's income was £2,200 per annum payable to the dowager.

13.   Ibid., annotation on DDM 11/69/22.

14.   Ibid., DDM 50/34.

15.   Parliamentary Papers 1831-1832 XXXIX, *Parliamentary Boundary Commissioners, Report and Plans*, 1832, Part III, 57.

16.   Baines, *History of Liverpool*, 637.

17.   For older dismissive assessments of the 'unreformed' Corporation, see, for instance, Muir, *History of Liverpool*, 152, 309. Like Muir, most earlier historians of Liverpool thought of themselves as 'reformers', being often Liberals or Radicals and hence taking a Whiggish view of the past; as such they were inclined to make a contemporaneously 'politically-correct' rather than a detached assessment of the pre-1832 administration. There is as yet no adequate study of post-1750 Liverpool: in particular its social history and historical demography lack modern investigation of the sources. (See, however, a useful exploratory essay, Michael Power, 'The growth of Liverpool', in John Belchem, ed., *Popular politics, riot and labour: essays in Liverpool history 1790-1940*, Liverpool, 1992, 21-37.) Hence the general comments in the text that follow, being based only on contemporary insights, should be received with some caution.

18.   Muir, *History of Liverpool*. 279.

19.   Ibid., 281.

20.   Ibid., 272.

21.   Baines, *History of ... Liverpool*, 655. It is easy to see why restrictive covenants against letting the cellar as a separate dwelling and against the sale of alcohol came to be widely imposed in Liverpool on houses of any pretension to gentility.

22.   R. Brooke, *Liverpool as it was in the last quarter of the eighteenth century 1775-1800* (Liverpool, 1853), 453.

23.   R. Muir and E.M. Platt, *A history of the development of municipal government in Liverpool from the earliest times to the Municipal Reform Act, 1835* (London, 1906), 134.

24.   For evidence of muggings, etc, see *A Report of the Proceedings of a Court of Inquiry into the state of the Corporation of Liverpool ... 1833* (Liverpool, 1833), 54, 55.

25.   Muir and Platt, *Municipal government*, 134.

26.   Baines, *History of ... Liverpool*, 677.

27.   Ibid., 673.

28.   Ibid., 677.

82 *Fulwood Park*

29. *Report from the Select Committee on Town Holdings* (PP 1888 XXII), 482 (Qu. 11112).
30. Ibid., 483 (Qu. 11096).
31. Booth, 'Background', 38.
32. Picton, *Memorials*, 478.
33. From this combination of speculative development and public philanthropy, Paxton went on to lay out Birkenhead Park, the first park to be provided at public expense for the pleasure of its townspeople: J. McInniss, *Birkenhead Park* (Liverpool, 1984), 13.
34. See, for instance, *The Liverpool Courier and Commercial Advertiser*, 1 October 1845 and 21 January 1846.
35. C. Kerr, *St.Michael's Hamlet, Liverpool* (Liverpool, 1984) 3, and map of Toxteth in 1835.
36. An Old Stager, *Liverpool a few years since* (3rd ed., Liverpool, 1835), 49.
37. Lancashire County Record Office, Sefton MSS, DDM 50/39, licence to Mr Thomas Balmer, farmer of Aigburth Hall, to assign over to Mr William Bunnell, Butcher of Liverpool, 'all leasehold interest of all that messuage and tenements and land situate in Toxteth Park known as the White House farm held by one Indenture of Lease for one life by Thomas Balmer containing 14 acres and twenty perches of land customary measure and also to assign to William Bunnell the leasehold interest of five other closes of land held by the said Thomas Balmer by another Indenture of Lease for three lives all in being (himself, brother and son) premises adjoining the White House farm 9 acres, two roods and twenty-two perches subject to covenants therein provided that when William Bunnell enters, Thomas Balmer or William Bunnell pay £53.11s.8d. as a fine or consideration as is usually paid by my other tenants, commonly called an admittance fine or a fine for the tenant's right, otherwise the licence shall be void.' By the time of his death in 1833 Butcher Bunnell was described as 'gentleman'.
38. Griffiths, *History of Toxteth*, 125. After leasing to Thomas Balmer the White House farm, in 1781 Lord Sefton further leased the fields on which Fulwood Park was to be laid out. In 1803 these leases passed into the hands of William Bunnell (see previous note), who in 1808, obtained from the earl the freehold of this land, together with that of the White House. In 1833 William Bunnell died, leaving as his executors Thomas and William Birkett. These gentlemen in 1839 sold the White House to James Birkett and the fields in question to the Smiths. Griffiths obtained some of the above information from Ronald Stewart-Brown, a Liverpool solicitor who published numerous pieces on local history. The information accords with the title of Fulwood Park as set out in the recitals of later deeds, save that the

Birketts were apparently devisees on trust, the will having been proved by James Gill alone in 1834. The full covenants are set out in the Appendix below.

39. *Gore's Directory* [hereafter *Gore*], 1818, 267.

40. Lancashire County Record Office: O/42.

41. E. Baines, *History and directory of Liverpool 1824*, (Liverpool, 1824), 236.

42. *Gore*, 1841, 426;1845, 483; 1847, 553; 1851, 525.

43. *Gore*, 1853, 554.

44. Conveyance by lease and release was the usual form until the Conveyance by Release Act of 1841 made the lease itself unnecessary. Conveyance by Release alone continued until the passing of the Real Property Act of 1845.

45. Title deeds and documents: Trustees of Fulwood Park.

46. There is room for speculation about the original extent of the gate end of Fulwood Park, in two aspects. First, the line of present-day Aigburth Road seems to take a wider sweep to the north than in the nineteenth century and it is uncertain whether the additional sliver of land was part of the covenant scheme. Secondly, there is uncertainty about the site of the 'White House'. The executors of the purchaser of the relevant area of Toxteth Park from Lord Sefton, Thomas and William Birkett, in 1839 sold part of the land, the 'White House', to James Birkett. Until its demolition in 1935 this house was one of the oldest in Toxteth Park (D.M. Whale, *Lost villages of Liverpool*, Prescot, 1984, 51). It is shown on an estate plan of 1769 as 'New House Farm', but since the house was of stone, rendered and painted white, by the early nineteenth century it was known as 'White House Farm'. However, it was also confusingly known as 'Three Sixes' because of its inscribed date, 1666 (Booth, 'Background', 34). The Fulwood Park archive contains a copy of a deed dated 23 July 1845 - the same date as the conveyance to Hugh McNeile and in similar terms - conveying to James Birkett a plot in the park bounded on the east by another plot already owned by Birkett. From the plan on this deed it appears that the site of the 'White House' was the land already owned by Birkett before the creation of the park. Hence it was most probably in respect of the additional land purchased in 1845 that he signed the articles (unfortunately separate dates for the signatures of individual purchasers, shown in the case of Cressington Park, are not shown in this case.) Whether the 'White House' area was part of the original plan for the estate is therefore unclear. However, the land owned by Birkett shown on the 1847 tithe map, including that on which the 'White House' then stood (land shown on the map as part of that entitled 'Three Sixes'), appears to be included in the layout of lots on the plan annexed to the 1840 Articles.

47. Not including modern 'infill' building.

48. See the Appendix for the covenants.

49.   *Gore*, 1834, 274; 1862, 212.

50.   *Gore*, 1827, 123; 1839, 158; 1853, 212

51.   Possibly they were prospective purchasers who did not complete their purchases, and perhaps Holt acquired his land from one of them.

52.   C.G.Powell, *An economic history of the building industry 1815-1979* (London, 1980), 12.

53.   Auction particulars: Picton Library, Liverpool, Hf.333.33BRA. With regard to the builders, the report of the funeral of Samuel Holme noted that he entered the Town Council in 1842 and was Mayor in 1852; he was 'placed by Lord Palmerston on the list of borough magistrates'; was 'upright, sincere and liberal' and an energetic supporter of charitable institutions, particularly those connected with the Church of England'. His brother, James, buried on 14 October 1871, was a builder and contractor 'on a large scale; also one of the directors of the Lancashire and Yorkshire Railway Company, and director of the Royal Insurance Office'. He, too, was a member of the Town Council. Anon., *In Memoriam or funeral records of Liverpool celebrities* (Liverpool, 1876), 112, 114.

54.   Griffiths, *History of ... Toxteth*, 125.

55.   A. Moscardini, *Buildings of Liverpool* (Liverpool, 1978), 185.

56.   Samuel Holme was President of the Liverpool Athenaeum 1847-1848 and John Eden was Honorary Treasurer in 1846-1849. The membership records of the Athenaeum do not supply addresses so that it is not possible to be certain that Holme, Eden, and the others are in all instances the same men who signed the Deed. No similar Athenaeum association appears in relation to Grassendale or Cressington Parks (although there were other clubs).

57.   P.H. Williams, *A gentleman's calling - the Liverpool attorney-at-law* (Liverpool, 1980), 122. Joshua Lace was the first president of the Liverpool Law Library Society on its formation in 1827, and his son, Ambrose, was a later president.

58.   Legal connections throughout the affair are easy to detect. John Eden, a purchaser resident in the Park by 1861, attended the first meeting of the Law Library Society in 1827 when Ambrose Lace's father was elected president, and was himself its vice-president and president in 1829. Ibid, 185 and Appendix O.

59.   Ibid., Appendix O.

60.   1847 tithe map; 1851 census return.

61.   In 1861, the family were at home: Hugh McNeile, now 65, originally from Ireland, rector of St Paul's, Princes Park, his wife, 58, with one son and one daughter still at home and now with three grand-daughters and one grandson. The family seem to have moved shortly afterwards as they do not appear in *Gore* for 1862.

62.　　　The sixth head of household was a widow and annuitant.

63.　　　*Halsall v. Brizell* [1957] Ch 169.

6: Liverpool Park Estates: (2) Grassendale Park

The other two developments with which this study is concerned also lie to the east of the earlier town but beyond the boundaries of Toxteth Park and a good two miles further out than Fulwood Park, in 'Aigburth within Garston' as the township was described in early abstracts.[1] The earliest mention of the two separate hamlets of Aigburth and Garston is in the Coucher Book of Whalley Abbey compiled at the end of the thirteenth century, and both were named in the survey of the possessions of the abbey taken after the dissolution.[2] Following that, the land in the area seems to have remained in Crown hands before being bestowed on the hospital of the Savoy and hence being later referred to as the 'Savoy lands.' Large parts were eventually acquired by the Tarleton and Blackburne families, but the site of the two park estates, Grassendale and Cressington, lies between the lands of these two substantial purchasers.[3]

The site of Cressington Park was sold in January 1777 by Topham Beauclerk, holder by Letters Patent of the surviving Savoy lands, now deeply in debt.[4] After passing through several hands it was conveyed in 1812 to William Hope of Liverpool, gentleman, for a total purchase price of £22,000.[5] Hope's executors were holding it in the early 1830s. The site of the other park, neighbouring Cressington Park but slightly nearer town, Grassendale Park, was conveyed in 1775 to Thomas Hatton of Warrington, chapman, and eventually, after passing through several hands, was conveyed in 1814 to Arnold Harrison. In September 1835 Harrison sold part of his total purchase to the executors and trustees of the will of Thomas Banning deceased, sometime Postmaster of Liverpool. The executors were Thomas Haines Banning M.D., and William Banning, both of Liverpool, and the Reverend Benjamin Banning of Croft within Winwick. But in December 1838 the Bannings conveyed to John Woolwright, silk mercer of Liverpool, for £6,000, a parcel of land by the river of about 20 acres statute measure. At the same time, they also conveyed to him the interest in the strand they had obtained from Harrison.[6]

The question of the manorial rights of the area and hence the rights over the strand of the River Mersey from Otterspool up to Garston, which included the section at the Grassendale and Cressington sites, had been the subject of protracted dispute. In 1779 the Mayor, Alderman and Burgesses of Liverpool purchased the manorial rights of Garston, intending to regulate the fisheries in the river. 'Their intentions, however, like some of those avowed by their successors, appear to have been speedily abandoned.'[7] In 1780, they disposed of the manor to Peter Baker and John Dawson in equal moieties: having paid £1,950 they sold for £2,387.[8] The conveyance to Baker and Dawson had been subject to certain provisos and restrictions, and with certain reservation all of which were surrendered in February, 1785. After 1799 these rights were held by John Blackburne. The strand near Otterspool was enclosed in 1780 and a snuff mill erected. In 1816, a Mr Moss, who owned the land adjacent to the Otterspool strand, compromised an action with the then holder of the manorial rights, Blackburne, and paid him £500 for the rights to the strand.[9] Subsequently, other land owners along the river bought their rights, in order to begin embanking against erosion, and Harrison at Grassendale was one of these. In practice, at this stage the only effective embanking work seem to have been done by Moss who erected a stone-paved slope mainly above high-tide mark.

At the time of a survey of the Port of Liverpool in 1828, the lands of Messrs. Hope and Woolwright were referred to thus:

> *The Executors of the late William Hope, Esq. Land.* The land is open to the shore, and suffers much from the effect of the tide; about 15 yds. in width is supposed to have been destroyed within the last twenty years. Mr. Hope's executors state the strand was purchased long before the late Mr. Blackburne became possessed of the manor, and claim to low water mark.

> *John Woolwright. Land.* This land having no protection from the tide suffers greatly. The strand in front purchased by Mr. Woolwright.[10]

It seems that by the late 1830s Hope and the Woolwright estate owned the whole frontage to the Mersey from the northern boundary of the Blackburne property to the southern boundary of the Tarleton purchase, and from the river eastward to the limits of Garston hamlet.

The Garston area was in the nineteenth century subject to the operation of several 'land companies'. The park estates to be discussed were developed by unincorporated associations which called themselves 'land companies', Grassendale by the Aigburth Land Company and Cressington by the Second

Aigburth Land Company. As may be gathered from the names, there was a close association between these latter two developments, although each operated independently. But other parts of the area were developed by the Liverpool Land Company and the Garston Land Company. The former purchased Island Farm from Robert Lightbody in about 1864; this land in the south-eastern part of Garston (round Island Road) is now covered in terraced houses.[11]

Grassendale Park
In December 1838 John Woolwright purchased from the executors of Thomas Banning a parcel of land of 20 acres, 2 roods, 17 perches (a measurement that cannot be considered altogether accurate), this being land situated about four miles from the Liverpool Exchange.[12] He paid £6,000 for the land and on the same day also took a conveyance of the strand, for which he paid £1,000. Thus the price per acre was approximately £350. On 13 February 1839, Woolwright mortgaged the land to Henry Holmes and John Leyland, both Liverpool merchants, for £5,000. In March 1847 Woolwright died, but by an agreement in writing dated 1 November 1845 he had already agreed to sell the land for the sum of £10,500 to a group of purchasers: William Ockleston, James Rowan, Ralph Leyland, William Valiant Willis and John Starr de Wolf. The strand rights being included, about £500 per acre was paid on this occasion, a sharp increase on the acre price of seven years earlier. (It was not, however excessive, in the light of the statement of the 1832 Boundary Commissioners that at this earlier date £500 was not an infrequent price for land in 'very favourable situations' even as far as four miles from Liverpoool.) One reason for the increase in the value of the Garston land may have been that, commencing in 1831, horse omnibus services had extended to the Liverpool suburbs, a change which, according to a mid-Victorian local historian, 'enables thousands of persons, of moderate means, whose occupations are in Liverpool, to reside in the pleasant villages which encircle it, extending from Bootle to Aigburth.'[13] The entrance to Cressington Park came to be described as being within 300 yards of the omnibus station.[14] While most of the families who resided in the park estates no doubt travelled into town in their own carriages, an omnibus service was presumably of convenience to their servants and visiting small

tradesmen.

The 1845 purchase price was to be paid in ten instalments of £525, with interest at 4½%, the first payment to be made on 29 July 1846 and the last on 29 July 1849. In the event, payment appears to have been made by 9 March 1849, on which date the remainder of the land not yet conveyed to members of the Aigburth Land Company was vested in its trustees. By this date Woolwright had died and his estate was in the hands of his executors, John Pearce, silk mercer of Cockspur Street, Westminster, and James Radley, hotel-keeper of Liverpool; the mortgage had in August 1847 been assigned to James Dawson Rodick, subject to the equity of redemption; and after the bankruptcy of one of the 1845 purchasers, William Ockleston, the appointed assignees of his estate had agreed to sell his four shares in the Land Company to Ralph Leyland for £158.[15] The deed of conveyance to the trustees of 9 March 1849 was consequently made between the following individuals: Rodick (the mortgagee), Pearce and Radley (Woolwright's executors), Robert Ockleston, surgeon of Cheadle, Cheshire, Robert Knott Carter, merchant of Liverpool, and Charles Turner, Official Assignee of Liverpool (all three on behalf of the bankrupt Ockleston), William Ockleston himself, and the four other 1845 purchasers - James Rowan, gentleman, Ralph Leyland, plumber and glazier, William Valiant Willis, merchant of Liverpool, and John Starr de Wolf, also merchant of Liverpool. Even before the completion of the purchase and this conveyance, some plots had been conveyed by way of sub-sale to certain shareholders, Ralph Leyland, Joseph Seddon and Henry Gardner Ireland, names which subsequently figured prominently in the affairs of the park.

The Aigburth Land Company was formed by the agreement (under seal) of 1 November 1845 which contained a plan of the land, with roads, 85 plots, a river wall and a terrace. Pursuant to this was an indenture of 2 May 1846 (in which the contract with Woolwright is recited) made between Rowan, Leyland, Willis and de Wolf of one part and the subscribers to the deed of the other part -

> with a view and for the purpose of forming a society of persons who should become jointly interested in the said contract and amongst whom the property so agreed to be purchased should (subject to the provisions hereinafter mentioned) be allocated and

divided for the purpose of the erection thereon by such persons respectively for moderate sized villas for their own residences. The majority of the 54 subscribers to this deed were businessmen rather than 'gentlemen' and clearly the arrangements were not intended to be in the same class as those of Fulwood Park. Of the promoters of the scheme, William Ockleston was a hide merchant, appearing as such in trade and street directories from 1821 until 1857.[16] But he does not appear ever to have lived in Grassendale Park. Ralph Leyland made his first appearance in an 1835 directory, as a member of Leyland and Earle, plumbers, glaziers and painters of 10 Church Street. By 1849, Leyland's home was in Aigburth and by his last appearance in 1862 he had risen in society to become 'Ralph Leyland, Gentleman'.[17]

Grassendale Park appears under that name in the census return of 1851, by which date there were eleven residents (plus a gardener at the lodge), including Leyland, James Rowan, retired merchant, and Henry Ireland, furrier, formerly of 92 Bold Street.[18] James Rowan is first found in an 1841 directory and is already 'Gentleman'; he moved to Grassendale Park from Everton before 1849.[19] Willis and de Wolf remain mysteries; neither of them lived in the Park, nor did they sign the 1848 deed of covenant noted below. They subscribed for only one share each and did not sign the plan as plot holders.[20] Why and how they came to be trustees of the scheme are not known.

The 1846 indenture set out the terms on which the Aigburth Land Company was to operate; eighty-five shares were agreed upon, not all being subscribed for. Later applications were to be approved by the Committee of Management, such applicants being required to sign the agreement within two months of notification of acceptance from the Secretary. The sum of £3 per month was to be paid until £200 per share had been subscribed, or less if that turned out to be sufficient to meet the expenses already incurred. Shares might be forfeit if payments were two months in arrears: evidence of inheritance or marriage was to be delivered to the Secretary. John Woolwright was to be paid out of the Society's funds. A General Meeting was to be held at the Clarendon Rooms at 12 noon on 27 July 1846 and on every subsequent 27 July. Extraordinary General Meetings might be called by the trustees, at which a quarter of the shareholders would constitute a

quorum. The deed laid down the rules for the conduct of meetings, which
resemble those for the conduct of meetings of limited companies in their
requirements, for instance, that of notice to be given of certain types of
resolution.

As regards the physical planning of the park, once the land for roads
was reserved the residue was to be divided into lots, plans of which were to
be submitted to the shareholders. Drains, sewers and a sea wall were to be
installed and regulations imposed on the making of bricks and on building.
As shown above, the Company was working on the basis that it would
receive a total of 85 x £200 = £17,000, over five and a half years. The land
itself having cost £10,500, the sum of £6,500 was left to pay for work on the
site-roads, drains, the embankment and the promenade. As no minutes of
committee meetings are available for Grassendale Park, it is not possible to
examine the immediate outcome of this planning. Since the receipts of £255
per month would have brought in only £9,180 by the end of three years, it
seems likely that some shareholders paid in advance of call, possibly when
they were ready to build on their plot, so that they could take a conveyance
of it.

Pursuant to the setting up of the Company, a Deed of Covenant was
prepared for signature by the shareholders. This deed of 9 May 1848 recites
that restrictive covenants contained in the agreement with Woolwright were
to be put into all subsequent deeds. The deed was made between the several
subscribers (mostly the same as those who subscribed to the deed of
settlement noted above) and Rowan, Leyland, Willis, De Wolf and Rodick,
to whom monies were still owing. The full covenants are set out in the
Appendix to the present volume, but it may be noted here that only one house
was to be built on each plot of 1,000 sq.yds, and that the house was to be of
no more than two storeys and of no less value than £400, exclusive of fences
and outbuildings. No trade, manufacture or business was to be allowed and
examples of various noxious trades were specifically listed as banned. In this
context, it seems that running a small school or boardinghouse was not in the
early years considered contrary to this covenant. According to the 1851
census, one of the residents was Jane Milburn, together with her four
unmarried sisters, all teachers or retired teachers: in 1851 they had seven
pupils, in 1861 sixteen. Again, in 1851 Thomas Barber, clergyman, had three

pupils, while Ellen Knowles, boardinghouse keeper, had four Swiss lodgers.

Positive obligations to contribute to the maintenance of the roads, sea wall and terrace, and the main drains and sewers were also imposed, each plot owner being required to contribute a due and just proportion in respect of the plot or plots held by him, the current trustees being given a right of action to recover any sums unpaid. The parties to the deed agreed to abide by, submit to and observe all such reasonable and lawful rules and regulations made by the owners of plots at a meeting duly held, and pay any sums decided on by such meetings, not only for the maintenance of the roads, sewers, sea wall and promenade, but also for lighting the roads with gas.

The deed of covenant revised the 1846 rules about meetings in several respects, as follows. Henceforth there were to be two meetings a year, on the first Monday in March and September of each year; extraordinary meetings might be called by the trustees or by holders of twenty or more of the plots. Seven days' notice in writing was to be given of any meeting and, in the case of extraordinary meetings, the business for which it was convened was to be notified as well. Ten proprietors of at least twenty plots formed a quorum. Voting entitlement was basically one vote per plot, but the owner of two to five plots was given only two votes; six to nine plots, three votes; ten plots upwards, four votes. To guard against the packing of meetings at which, for instance, large expenditure might be sanctioned or rules revised to the disadvantage of some proprietors or to the financial advantage of others, no determination of any meeting was to be annulled or altered save by the determination of two successive subsequent meetings.[21] A minute book was to be kept; meetings could remove trustees, and the trustees were to stand seised of any plot unallotted, the lodge, roads, terrace and the rights of strand. This is basically how Grassington Park is still run. On the conveyance in March 1840 to the first trustees of the roads, etc., are endorsed deeds of appointment of new trustees in 1861, 1886, 1902, 1912, 1926, 1943 and 1947. Appointments are now made by separate deed but the continuity is unbroken.

Building proceeded at a fairly leisurely pace. In 1851, there were only eleven houses occupied, but, as noted earlier in respect of Fulwood Park, this did not mean a paucity of population, since some 108 individuals, inclusive

of children, servants and pupils, were resident in these households. Three
more houses were in the course of construction. By 1861, there were still
only eighteen occupied houses (but two gardeners and their families appeared
to live in separate dwellings); in 1871, the number of occupied houses
remained the same, although there were also seven unoccupied houses. The
1881 census recorded 22 main households, while in 1891 there were 33
households, plus the dwellings of lodge and park keepers, and two
unoccupied houses. Although the number of households was still less than
half the number of original plots, some residents had taken multiple plots, so
that by the end of the century it was probably the case that over half of the
park was actively occupied. The 1960s map of the conservation area indicated
that some forty houses were in the category considered worthy of
conservation, and this indicates that by the second half of the present century
there had been relatively little scope for modern infill building within the
original covenant scheme of one house per 1,000 square yard plot.

Grassendale Park is adjoined by the larger Cressington Park. But the
left-hand quarter of the oblong of the two Parks, between Grassendale Park
and Aigburth Road, is occupied by late-Victorian semi-detached houses along
roads called Western and Eastern Drive. This area is named on maps as
Woodend Park, after the property which formerly fronted Aigburth Road.
From the regularity of the building and the size of the plots, it appears to be
a later, more speculative development. The houses have restrictive covenants
but there is no overall scheme comparable to the schemes still operating in
respect of both Grassendale and Cressington Parks.

NOTES TO CHAPTER 6

1.   Much information on the early history of these pieces of land is available in J. Boult, 'The historical topography of Aigburth and Garston', *Transactions of the Historic Society of Lancashire and Cheshire*, 20, 1867-8, 147-90.

2.   Boult believes that Aigburth Old Hall was the abbot's grange. This was demolished circa 1840 but the outbuildings were left (ibid., 214). These form part of the house now known as Stanlaw Grange, supposed to be the oldest occupied residence in Liverpool.

3.   Boult was unable to learn when and why the freehold was alienated: Ibid., 174, 179.

4.   The Honorable Topham Beauclerk (1739-1780) - 'gay, dissipated Beauclerk', but a great friend of Dr. Johnson - was the only son of Lord Sidney Beauclerk and the grandson of the first duke of St. Albans (an illegitimate son of Charles II by Nell Gwyn). Lord Sidney married Mary Norris of Speke, near Liverpool, and after his death in 1744 and her death in 1766 the Garston properties of the Norris family passed to Topham Beauclerk. The Garston estates were probably already encumbered by Lady Mary's grandfather, Sir William Norris, a notorious spendthrift. Neither Lord Sidney nor Topham took care of the estate which was finally dismembered and sold from 1775 onwards: ibid., 165.

5.   Beauclark sold to the Reverend Joseph Bragg, of Mosley Vale, Wavertree. In 1805, Bragg bequeathed all the property to his nephew, Joshua Lucock, of Lorton Hall, Cumberland, provided that he took the name Joshua Lucock Bragg, this being done in May 1805. In March 1808, Lucock Bragg conveyed his interest to John Clerke of Ashfield for £13,000, and Clarke sold to Hope: Ibid., 178.

6.   The land passed to Hatton's daughter, who married Edward Wilson (one of their several children was a daughter married to John Clarke of Ashfield, West Derby, Mayor of Liverpool in 1809). In January 1808, the property passed from Mrs Wilson's representatives to Ashton Byrom of Liverpool, merchant, and in November 1814, Byrom conveyed his interest to Harrison: ibid., 174.

7.   Ibid., 167.

8.   Boult, 'Historical topography', suggests that the purchase by Baker and Dawson may have been a temporary investment for part of the proceeds of a well-known local privateering success. A vessel built by their yard had been rejected by the purchaser but it was fortunate enough in October 1778 to meet and capture the 'Carnatic', a French East Indiaman, a prize valued at £135,000. Mossley Hill Hall was erected out of the proceeds and for long was known by the derisive pseudonym of Carnatic Hall. However the name has persisted: the University of Liverpool halls of residence, now on the site, back on to Carnatic Road and are known as the

Carnatic Halls.

9.   The history of the strand after it passed into private possession is tangled and not altogether clear. In 1791, Baker and Dawson conveyed the manor to the executors of the will of Richard Kent deceased. Kent's estate was the subject of a private Act of Parliament to lift an entail; the act was obtained at the expense of John Blackburne, who in 1799 obtained a conveyance of, *inter alia*, the manor vested in the trustees. However, it seems that some doubt was later raised concerning the effectiveness of the 1780 'privatising' conveyance since in 1833 the Corporation of Liverpool executed a confirmatory conveyance to Harrison, then holding the Grassendale site, of the fee simple of the strand, with all the appurtenant manorial rights. Ibid., 168.

10.   Ibid., 161. Boult gives the date of the survey as 1828 and it notes Woolwright's purchase of the strand, but elsewhere the date of the purchase is given as 1838: I have not attempted to investigate the apparent discrepancy.

11.   Details of the operation of these companies are not known but the Garston company 'comprised some of the most influential gentlemen connected with the St Helens Canal and Railway Company': ibid., 170, 180 (citing title deeds of these companies for the history of the area).

12.   The account of the early history of this park is based on the title deeds in the possession of the Trustees of Grassendale Park; and on Boult, 'Historical topography', 174.

13.   T. Baines, *History of the commerce and town of Liverpool* (Liverpool, 1852), 629.

14.   *Liverpool Mercury and Lancashire General Advertiser*, 24 July 1846.

15.   Woolwright died at Ryde, Isle of Wright, to which location he had presumably retired. Ockleston's fiat of bankruptcy was dated 5 December 1845.

16.   *Gore's Directory* [hereafter *Gore*], 1821, 231; 1857, 173; 1862, 208. Despite his bankruptcy, the firm of William Ockleston and Son continued to be listed, but in 1857 the name of James Greaves Ockleston was joined to that of William and after 1862 the former was solely listed under the name fo the firm.

17.   *Gore*, 1835, 240; 1849, 352; 1862, 170. Earle does not appear at later dates.

18.   A Robert Lightbody also resided there, though not apparently a shareholder. This was perhaps the same Robert Lightbody who in 1864 was to sell Island Farm to the Liverpool Land Company, the land having been purchased from Topham Beauclerk by Robert's father, Adam Lightbody, a Liverpool merchant (Boult, *Aigburth and Garston*, 179).

19.   *Gore*, 1841, 406; 1849, 496.

20.   De Wolf appears in directories from 1843, Willis from 1845: *Gore*, 1843, 531; 1845, 560.

21.   A similar provision appeared in early Companies Acts.

7: Liverpool Park Estates: (3) Cressington Park

The history of the site of Cressington Park has been discussed in the previous chapters. The surviving records of the operation of the park are fuller than those of Grassendale Park and its history can therefore be discussed in greater detail.[1] In the matters of legal form and the individuals involved there has undoubtedly been a past connection between the two neighbouring parks, although unfortunately this cannot be fully traced because of the unequal survival of documentation.

Promotion and foundation of the scheme

No deed of settlement is available in the case of Cressington Park. On the other hand, early committee minutes have survived and provide much significant information. The earliest meeting minuted is the First General Meeting of the Second Aigburth Land Company on 20 October 1846, although by this date no equivalent of the deed of settlement of Grassendale Park had yet been executed. Of a still earlier date are the advertisements for the Company's scheme to be found in the local press. On 24 July the following advertisement appeared in the *Liverpool Mercury and Lancashire General Advertiser* under the heading SECOND AIGBURTH LAND COMPANY.

> The success attending the FIRST AIGBURTH LAND COMPANY has induced the Proprietors of the adjoining estate to bring their land forward on similar terms. The property now offered consists of about 41 acres extending from the Aigburth Turnpike Road to the River Mersey beautifully situated and about 4 miles from the Liverpool Exchange. The entrance is within 300 yards of the Omnibus station. The length of the river frontage is about 320 yards. It is designed that this land shall be divided amongst the members of a Society in 170-175 plots, of not less than 1,000 yards each. A plan has been prepared showing its capabilities for such division. Names of intending Members will be received by Mr. John Bennett, Estate Agent, Lord Street Chambers, where the plan may be seen and explanatory prospectuses may be had.

This advertisement was followed in the same journal by another of 7 August under the same heading.

Parties desirous of having shares in the above UNDERTAKING
are advised to make early application as nearly 100 shares are
already subscribed for. Applications to be made to .... [as before].

It will be recalled that the deed of settlement of Grassendale Park was dated
2 May 1846; it would seem that the contract to purchase the site of
Cressington Park from the estate of William Hope either followed swiftly on
the heels of the the the first moves of the Grassendale scheme, with their related
expectations of a successful outcome, or had been in contemplation even
before that.

The conveyance to the trustees of Cressington Park provides the
following information. William Hope jnr, in exercise of the power contained
in the will of William Hope snr, with the consent of Maria Jones, Peter Hope
and Harriet Jones, the only other surviving children of the testator, contracted
with Ralph Leyland, John Bennett, Joseph Angelus Dominic Watts and
Thomas Doran for the absolute sale to them *inter alia* of the land described
and conveyed, for £1,000 per Cheshire acre; and Leyland, Bennett, Watts
and Doran afterwards contracted with William Okell and Alexander
Colquhoun Jeffrey for the sale of the land to them for £24,658 5s. A
'Cheshire' acre (also sometimes called the large or customary measure) being
considerably larger than a statute acre, the purchase price is not so
extraordinary. The statute measure in the conveyance was 40 acres 3 roods
1 perch. The price per (normal) acre was about £600, compared with £500
in the same year in the case of Grassendale Park, making it likely that the
success to date of the earlier venture did precede this purchase and so enable
the vendors to get a better price.

Assuming that the advertisements are correct in saying that the terms of
shareholding were to be similar to those of the First Aigburth Land
Company, application of the share price in the deed of settlement of
Grassendale Park to the stated number of lots in Cressington Park gives the
following total financial return: 175 lots, the projected maximum, at £200 per
share, payable by instalments, producing £35,000. Deducting from this the
purchase price of the land, £24,658 5s, leaves a sum of £10,341 15s for the
construction of roads, drains, the sea wall, promenade, and other common
facilities. However, in the event the land was divided into only 174 lots and
three of these were given for the construction of a church, St Mary's,

Grassendale. The price of a lot in Cressington Park was £144 4s, compared with £123 10s in Grassendale Park. Monthly pay days should, therefore, have produced £513 or half-yearly receipts of £3,078. This figure accords quite well with the recorded payments of half-yearly instalments of the purchase price to the vendors, a similar arrangement to that in respect of Grassendale Park having been agreed. The purchase price with interest at about 5% was paid by 5 March 1851, at least five and a half years after the contract to purchase. The sum of £75 was retained pending the resolution of a minor dispute which arose as to the measurement of the land, although this was finally settled on the original terms. The conveyance of the land to the trustees was executed on 3 May 1851. In addition to paying for the land, the sea wall had also been completed by this time, at a cost of about £2,000.[2]

The whole scheme took longer to get under way than Grassendale Park, possibly because from the start there was a more commercial air about it. In the extant documents there is no recital equivalent to that in the documents for Grassendale Park stating that the purpose was to build residences for the proprietors, although there may have been one in the missing deed of settlement. That such a deed was executed appears from the minutes; on 5 January 1847, John Jones, appointed solicitor to the company at the first committee meeting following the first general meeting, was instructed to prepare a deed. This was done, and after the deed was approved by Mr Crook of Counsel, it was resolved that it should be available for signature by the shareholders at Mr Jones' office on South John Street on Monday and Tuesday, 10 and 11 May 1847.[3]

The proprietors bringing this land forward for development were Leyland, Bennett, Watts and Doran. Ralph Leyland has already appeared as one of the prime movers in the Grassendale Park scheme. John Bennett, as the advertisements indicate, was an estate agent. He made his first appearance in a street directory in 1839 and continued in business in Lord Street Chambers until at least 1857.[4] His son, John Bennett jnr, joined him in the business and was elected secretary of the Second Aigburth Land Company with a remuneration of £40 per annum. Joseph Angelus Dominic Watts, a printer, appeared in the directory as a wood engraver in 1837; by 1843, his address was given as 7, Mary Ann Street, Everton, the same address as that of Leyland. Since Leyland was given as the occupier in the directory, it seems probable that Watts lodged with Leyland. By 1851, Watts' address was given as Grassendale Park, at which time he employed eight men.[5] Although not appearing as a resident in the 1861 census, he did appear in 1871, being by then a printer employing 62 men, women and boys. Watts was a signatory of both the deed of settlement and the deed of covenant of Grassendale Park. In respect of Cressington Park, he signed the plan and deed of covenant, taking three double plots, and possibly a fourth, since in 1856 he transferred half to a William Kershaw, also of Cressington Park. Thomas Doran, a book-keeper, listed in the directory from 1829, operated from Falkner Street for 20 years, being retitled in 1843 as 'accountant'[6]. He seems to have had no financial or residential connection with the park, although he served as a committee member until October 1851. Thus the promoters appear to have been either active businessmen with a commercial interest in the scheme or else straw men who offered other services than financial ones.

John Jones, mentioned above, was the solicitor who acted for the promoters of both the Grassendale and Cressington schemes. Jones, who appears in the Law List between 1840 and the 1860s, does not seem to have been among the leaders of the local profession, but given the close involvement of Liverpool attorneys in building developments of the previous century, it is possible that he was instrumental in bringing together the consortia which financed the parks. In 1855, signatures on the deeds are witnessed by Robert Jones, clerk to J. Jones. Robert Jones enters the Law List in 1860, when further signatures on the deed of covenant are attested by him as 'solicitor' and later by clerks of Robert Jones - the Jones family appear to have been a dynasty of attorneys. It is unclear whether the local example of Fulwood Park formed a precedent for the legal form of the schemes to which John Jones was advisor, or whether such schemes were so widespread nationally that the acceptable form was well known to all solicitors. Precedent books in their modern style do not set out relevant documentary forms until rather later. Nevertheless, if evidence in cases is to be believed, the use of deeds of mutual covenant was common, and from the instance of Fulwood Park it seems that the best respected attorneys in Liverpool had faith in their efficacy.

Further evidence that Cressington Park was a more speculative development, which therefore took longer to set in motion, is provided by the fact that, whereas the deed of covenant of Grassendale Park was signed on 9 May 1848, only two years after the deed of settlement of 2 May 1846, it was not until 18 August 1851 that a deed of covenant was signed between the purchasers of plots in Cressington Park and the trustees, the deed of settlement having apparently been signed on 10/11 May 1847, four years and four months earlier. The conveyance to the trustees of the outstanding land in Cressington Park took place on 3 May 1851, although it was not until the committee meeting of 21 May that Jones was able to report that the vendors had signed the conveyance. In contrast, the deed of covenant on Grassendale Park was most likely signed by all parties at more or less the same date (since individual signings are not separately dated), and the date of the deed precedes the date of the conveyance of the outstanding land to the trustees.

At a committee meeting on 4 June 1851, Jones handed to the committee the deed of conveyance of the estate and it was resolved that any shareholder might take up his title on payment of the balance due, together with a promissory note for a sum calculated on the basis of £5 per lot, the promised total to meet any contingencies that might thereafter arise. Committee meetings had already been held on 7 and 10 May to consider the draft form of the covenants to be put before a General Meeting of the shareholders, for incorporation into a deed of covenant. The general meeting was held on 5 June when the form of covenants was adopted. As will be seen hereafter, the form was basically very similar to that adopted for Grassendale Park. Once the covenant scheme had been agreed, the deed was engrossed. The signatures commence with that of George Hill, builder, dated 19 August 1851, but the dates of the other 89 signatures are spread over nearly twenty years, the last being that of John Davies, book-keeper, on 11 July 1870. A plan of the estate as lotted was also signed by each purchaser and, with a single exception, it is possible to identify from this plan the land purchased by each member of the association.[7]

Most of the purchasers took one or two lots only, but there were instances of multiple purchase. Ralph Leyland has already been noted as one of these purchasers. John Bennett signed the deed of covenant three times, the first time in November 1851, when six lots (five adjoining) were taken. The subsequent signatures in July 1859 and January 1860 may, however, be those of his son, John Bennett jnr., these signatures being in relation to purchases of two single lots auctioned by the company, one in Bennett's sole name and one jointly with a William Vaughan of Bradford. Of other multiple purchasers, Abraham Horsfall, who signed the deed of covenant for Grassendale Park but who does not seem to have lived there (at least not in census years), signed the deed and plan of Cressington Park twice, for a total of seven lots (perhaps eight - Horsfall signed for numbers 169-172 but there is no number 171 on the plan). According to the 1871 census his residence was 1, Cressington Park, probably a house built on the double lot, numbers 1 and 2, on the river front. When he signed for these lots in January 1852, he was described as a boot and shoe manufacturer; by 1871, aged 72, he was a 'gentleman'.[8] In 1881, he still lived in the park, was a retired millwright, and the house number was 4. (One of the difficulties of tracing the history of any particular house is that quite frequent renumbering occurred as the park was developed). Shand and Myers (forenames illegible), merchants, jointly signed for four double lots and Edward Evans took three double lots; James Roche, master mariner, took two double lots, as did William Gillespie and William Gillespie jnr. Another large purchaser was J.A.D. Watts who held three double lots and one single lot. Among individuals already mentioned, William Ockleston, the bankrupt hide merchant, also took a double plot, although he does not appear to have lived in Cressington Park, any more than he did at Grassendale. H.G. Ireland took a double plot but did live in Grassendale Park. Walter Bostock, boot and shoe manufacturer, signed the deed of covenant of Grassendale Park but had become a resident of Cressington Park by 1861, the first time the park appears in the census returns. Joseph Wilson, warehouseman, a shareholder in Grassendale Park, took a single plot in Cressington (the only possible clue to its location is that in the 1871 census, Eliza Wilson, gentleman's widow, lived at 31 Cressington Park).

The trustees to whom the land was conveyed in 1851 were William Okell and Alexander Colquhoun Jeffrey. Okell, a silk merchant, first appears in the directories in 1834 as a silk mercer and linen-draper at 10 Paradise Street.[9] His later larger establishment, the 'Beehive' at 17/19 Paradise Street, selling straw bonnets and carpets in addition to textile material and curtains, was regularly and prominently advertised, for instance in the

Liverpool Mercury of 3 July 1846. Jeffrey was a surgeon practising from 1827 for about 30 years. Most of that time, he lived at 9 Queen Street, but latterly in Princes Park.[10]

Okell and Jeffrey, together with James Ingram, Robert Ballantyne and James Rowan, had been elected trustees at the first general meeting of the Second Aigburth Land Company held at the Clarendon Rooms on 20 October 1846. All were also members of the committee, but some or all were frequently recorded as absent from committee meetings. The chosen first president of the Society was Thomas Cooke, and the treasurer William Warren Smith. The elected committee had as additional members James Fisher Jones, George Summers, Ralph Leyland, Thomas Doran, William Hutton, Henry Gardner Ireland, John Tyrer, John Bennett snr, John Jones and William Ockleston (many of whom have been discussed above). The appointed secretary was John Bennett jnr. It was proposed at the meeting that no remuneration out of the society's funds should be paid to the trustees or the committee, but instead it was resolved that this should be left to the committee to decide. Two other resolutions were carried; that the division of the lots of land, when it occurred, should take place by ballot, and that each member should have only one vote. The original motion proposed by two of the committee members had been that each member holding more than one share should have two votes, but this attempt to bias the system in favour of the multiple holders was defeated, perhaps indicating that sufficient single-lot holders were present. The number of members attending is in fact not recorded; the only names mentioned other than the ones listed above were those of Henry Davison and John Davies, the members who proposed and seconded the successful amendment to the resolution on voting rights.

At the first meeting of the committee on 22 October John Jones was appointed solicitor and instructed to prepare a draft contract for the transfer of the land from the promoters to the trustees, and a draft was presented to the committee on 3 November. A sub-committee of Hutton, Okell and Cooke was appointed to meet with the trustees at Jones' office to peruse the draft, and a Committee of Works was also appointed, Bennett, Ireland, Doran, Okell, Leyland, Tyrer, Smith and Cooke being the members. At a subsequent meeting on 1 December it was decided that the contract from Hope and Jones to Leyland and the others, and the contract from them to the trustees, should be submitted to Mr Crook for his opinion. On 5 January 1847 it was reported that Crook had approved the contracts, that the trustees had signed, and that the bank accounts had been transferred to their names. A notice of the contract was to be served on Mr Hope. As mentioned previously, a deed of settlement was then prepared, and 300 abstracts were ordered to be printed once it had been signed, for distribution to the members at a charge of 6d each. (It would be surprising if all of these had disappeared, but if any still exist they are presumably in individual sets of deeds). The first problem that arose for the trustees was the bankruptcies of two of their number, Ingram and Ballantyne, towards the end of 1848. In consequence of this, it was necessary to get a conveyance from them immediately. Jones again consulted Crook, who said that such a deed could not be proceeded with until the ballot had been held for the lots of land. It was therefore resolved that the plan, decided on in June 1847, should now be lithographed and 300 copies distributed among the members.

A general meeting on 3 January 1849 confirmed the committee's proposal that the ballot should take place on 7 February, and also agreed rules for the ballot, as follows. (1) The plan now produced by the surveyor as correct was to be considered official for the purposes of balloting; (2) The chairman, secretary and two members of the committee should record officially to whom lots were awarded; (3) The name of each member should be written on a card, with the number of lots he was entitled to. (4) Holders of more than one lot could have either each lot on a separate card or else two lots (but not more) on a single card. (5) Absent parties could have their cards filled in by the secretary. (6) The cards would be placed in a ballot box and drawn out by a disinterested person; the lots from 1 to 174 would be allotted in the order drawn. After the ballot, no work was to be done on any lot without the consent of the committee, who reserved to themselves the right to take or add sand, gravel, or other material, and to fill up the pits on the land, which was to be levelled within three months. Any buildings already on the land were to be the property of the company and not of the member on whose land they stood.

At a further committee meeting on 7 February it was resolved that the five lots belonging to the company should be drawn in two double lots and one single lot. The ballot duly took place at a general meeting held after this committee meeting but no details of it are recorded in the minutes. The matter of the release of the bankrupt trustees could now proceed, but this involved negotiations with various parties.[11] Eventually, on 2 July 1850, Jones was able to report that the release was duly signed and available to be deposited in the fire-proof box purchased by the committee in 1846. Jones' bill in this matter was £38; after some discussion, he agreed to accept £25.

By this time, James Rowan, who was in a very delicate state of health, was agreeable to resigning his trusteeship provided that the company returned the amount paid on his lot. Hence, in 1851 when the conveyance was executed, only two of the original trustees remained. Jones offered to draw up the draft conveyance to the trustees for £20. It was resolved that a deputation (Summers, Woods and Ireland) should wait upon the vendors to see whether they would bear any part of the expense; they would not.

Site preparation and building works
Grace's Farm, when purchased for development, was a 'greenfield' site. But unlike the site of Grassendale Park, which was described in the deeds as being 'laid out as one field or enclosure', the site of Cressington Park was composed of a dozen or so fields, some larger than others, with patches of woodland or scrub, ponds, pits and farm buildings. The whole preparation of the site had to be organised by the Committee of Works appointed, as noted above, at the first committee meeting on 20 October 1846. The general committee further resolved that a premium should be offered for the best plan for laying out the land; that the first prize should be 25 guineas, the second prize 5 guineas. The offer was to be advertised once in each Liverpool newspaper. The Committee of Works was to supervise the building of the sea wall, brickmaking, and other site preparations, and was empowered to let any part of the land they should think proper. By 1 December four tenders for brickmaking had been received; the bricks were to be made on the land itself using the materials to hand.[12] The tender accepted was that of a Mr Rowson, who would make the bricks for 14s 10d per thousand, but since he refused to count them out of the kiln, a tender was also accepted from P. Kenna to count them for 21s 8d. The land had meanwhile been measured by a Mr Young at 197,266 [sq.] yds. and an appointment had been made with a Captain Evans to advise on the construction of the sea wall. Finally, it was

agreed that, until the site was ready for house building, the land should be let to the farmer, Grace, on the best terms the sub-committee could arrange. Evans approved the line for the sea wall as proposed by the committee, and plans were put before the meeting of 1 April 1847 by James Fairclough for the building of the wall, together with a rival estimate from James Routledge for building to that plan but one foot thicker. The contract was awarded to Routledge for £1,775, the work to be superintended by a Mr Langsdale for £30. Out of the plans submitted for the lay-out of the estate the committee chose Plan 6. These committee recommendations were accepted by the members at a general meeting on 11 June, and the secretary forwarded the plan to Henry Summers for him to give the measurements of the respective lots, together with a copy of Young's survey. No details are recorded about the entrants to the lay-out competition, nor is the name of the winner stated; but since it was resolved that 25 guineas be paid to Summers he presumably was the winner and this is why he was later invited to submit plans for the entrance lodge.[13] The plan received from Summers showed the lots supposedly of 1,000 square yards, but when it was examined by Langsdale he claimed that several of them were 'greatly deficient', as a result of which opinion it was resolved that one of the 175 lots should be struck out.[14] A contract was made with a Mr Dyer to back up the sea wall for £130. On 5 October, the sub-committee reported that it had entered into an arrangement with a Mr Gray to draw a plan, but confirmation was postponed for one month.

Hints of cash flow problems had begun to appear. On 2 November 1847 it was resolved that £115 3s 0d in excise duty should be paid (for the bricks), that Kenna should be paid the balance of £23 17s 9d for the brickmaking, and that Routledge be paid the balance due to him for the sea wall out of 'tomorrow's' receipts. The following meeting again resolved to pay Routledge's outstanding arrears from the following day's receipts. Resolutions now began to appear regarding arrears of payments due from members; on 30 November it was resolved that Messrs. Gould, Davies and J. Fairclough were to be informed that unless arrears were paid up on or before the next pay-day, 5 January next, their shares would be forfeited. It was also agreed that parties paying subscriptions in advance would be allowed interest at 5% per annum. At the January 1848 committee meeting six other members were named as being in arrears, and at the same meeting it was reported that an arrangement had been made with the vendor, Hope, to let £2,000 of the £3,314 due to be paid remain over at 5%. Hope had also agreed to permit brickmaking to be postponed for another season. This relieved the membership from deciding at this early stage how many bricks they would want in 1848, and therefore from paying for them in instalments from December 1847, as had been resolved on 2 November 1847.

The general meeting of 20 January 1848 accepted the amended plan presented by Gray, and agreed that consideration of the ballot should be postponed for three months. Thus the ballot eventually took place in February 1849, but no major work was undertaken on the site until the end of 1850, virtually all the monthly receipts having gone to Hope for the purchase of the land, which had meanwhile been let to Grace's widow for two further yearly periods. A count made in May 1849 showed that 1,098,080 bricks had been made and that 156,530 had been removed. Requests from Doran for soil to fill in some of the pits on the land of the First Aigburth Land Company and from Watts for 500 bricks (probably for use in the building of his house in Grassendale Park, where he was resident by 1851) were not acceded to. It should be borne in mind that several of those involved in the Cressington preparations were also involved in the operations at Grassendale Park, where they were intending to live. Although Doran does not seem to have lived in either park, he evidently had some connection with Grassendale since he was forwarding a request on that company's behalf.

In July 1850 the committee resolved that possession of the land should be taken in September with a view to commencing work on the site in February 1851. Possession was obtained from Mrs Grace, the farm house and outbuildings henceforth to be let weekly if the Committee of Works thought proper. The time for laying out the land had arrived. On the recommendation of Watts, the secretary wrote to Mr Bolton of Ulverston, near Keswick, a surveyor. After viewing the site, Bolton wrote a letter which was put before the committee on 2 October 1850.

Gentlemen,
 I beg to offer my services on the following terms; I will engage to survey, calculate and relot all the lots of land as shown on the plan furnished including lay out all levels of the roads, take

all levels, draw up all specifications, superintend the making and placing of all sewers, roads, etc. and every other kind of work you may wish me to transact in the capacity of surveyor. When your works commence, I agree to be continually on the ground for the term of six to seven months and honestly and faithfully serve you. In consideration of which you are to pay me the sum of £80. At any time should you wish to discontinue my services, I agree to take my discharge and such compensation as you may deem correct.

> I remain etc.
>
> J. Bolton

Bolton was engaged to re-survey and stake out the plots as near to 1,000 square yards as possible, leaving the roads as shown on the plan, and a gratuity of £20 was offered if the work was completed to the entire satisfaction of the committee. By 4 December Bolton had completed his survey and produced a plan showing 172 lots, drawing attention to the fact that his survey showed 2,208 sqare yards less than that of Young. He also proposed preliminary work on the site, which he thought would have saved him 'a fortnight of hard labour' if it had been done before he had commenced work on the estate, and which would be likely to be of similar advantage to future contractors:

> to rid up all the fences on the Estate, throw the top of the fence into the ditch, level all up and burn the brush and other useless matter. Also take down all the trees which have to be removed from the line of the streets - dress up and put new soil into the roots of all those that must remain. This will, in my opinion, very much improve the Estate and give it a beautiful and park-like appearance.

Bolton's contractor estimated £25 for this work, but the committee hired Robert Bleasdale to do it for £18.

On 1 January 1851 Bolton's detailed specifications were put before the committee for -

> Works to the Estate called Grace's Farm situate at Aigburth in the Parish of Childwall; the said works comprise the making and finishing of approximately 2,160 lineal yds. of Brick Sewers, also

making and finishing of approximately 14,500 superficial yds. of rock pavement as specified below. Details of the work to be done to the esplanade, to make it similar to that of Grassendale Park, for the sewers and roads, and for 'macadamising' them, were also given. The contract was advertised in the Liverpool papers and by 20 January thirty tenders had been received, twenty local and fourteen from the Wirral. Ten from the lower end of the cost range were selected for further investigation by the Committee of Works. The highest tender, from Joseph Nickson of Toxteth, had been for £7,318 all inclusive; the selected tenders were all under £2,750. After 'minute examination and perusal of testimonials', the committee recommended to a general meeting that the tender of Thomas Abram of 15, Rose Vale, at a cost of £2,944 inclusive of curb stones and channels, be accepted.[15] This was passed unanimously. It was then resolved that a financial statement should be made forthwith and forwarded to each member, the statement to contain particulars of past expenditure and an estimate of future outlay, and also intimating a probable time of completion. The conveyance of the estate, however, had yet to be completed; there was a delay while agreement was reached on the question of measurement between Young, on behalf of the vendors, and Bolton for the company. The conveyance was signed on 3 May and on 16 April Bolton reported that work was progressing favourably.

The financial statement requested was read to and approved by the shareholders at a general meeting on 16 April 1851. The committee then also sought and were given power to complete the promenade, erect a lodge, entrance gates, pillars, lamp-posts, and any other common facilities, and to complete the whole of the communal works. A contract was now advertised for the completion of the promenade and this contract was also awarded to Abram for £320, having been negotiated down from £390, and Henry Summers was invited to submit plans for a lodge, not to exceed £400 in total cost. The Gas Company had already been approached, but had recommended waiting until the roads were properly consolidated and a number of villas erected before pipes were laid, since the company would have to pay rates from the date when the pipes were laid. Only in the printed account of the 1856 annual general meeting was it was reported that water and gas had now been introduced into the estate.

Abram's account for the roads and sewers was received in September 1851; the total was £3,297 8s 3d of which £2,250 had been paid on account. It was resolved that the balance should be paid as soon as funds permitted, and that Bolton should receive his £20 gratuity and also an extra £25 for the 'considerable time longer' which he had been detained with the works.[16] In October, Abram was paid £400 on account, but his attention was drawn to the roads, parts of which had sunk with recent heavy rain. An attempt was made to persuade Abram to allow a discount of 5% from his bill, but he refused, arguing that if the contract had been profitable he would have done so, but it had not been so, and he had already done a great deal of extra work which was more than equivalent. However, he agreed to make good the damage from the late rains. It was then resolved that he be invited to repair Mr Astley's wall, a wall which Astley alleged had been interfered with by the sinking of a stone quarry for the company's works. The committee resolved that Abram be authorised to rebuild the wall at a cost of 1s 6d per yard, the total not to exceed £20. (The figure of £20 is often mentioned in committee resolutions because the authorization of a general meeting was required for expenditure of a sum above this figure.)[17] Abram was paid by 3 March 1852, after giving an undertaking to repair the roads and wall by 1 June. However, by May 1854 Astley had grown weary of waiting and presented a bill for £39 7s 2d in respect of repairs to the wall which he had himself arranged to be done. Astley was requested to pay the bill, the company agreed to reimburse him when it was in funds, and Abram was requested to pay the company. In April 1855, the Company accepted £20 from Abram in settlement of the claim.

The entrance lodge had meanwhile been built to a plan approved by a general meeting of 19 December 1851.[18] By October 1852 the building was put into the hands of John Bennett for letting; but in March 1858 it was reported as having been untenanted since November last, dry rot having been found in the floors and joists which had then to be repaired at a cost of £21 15s 4d. The laying out of the entrance to the estate with gates, and the fitting of an iron railing to the promenade matching that at Grassendale Park, completed the basic programme of works to be done by the company.

Disputes and development

The main tasks had been completed by the end of 1851, and now that five years had passed since pay-days commenced, the company had received most of the money which it could expect in respect of the shares. However, the company was not having an easy time financially and the committee was seeking to recover all arrears on shares. A number of disputes, minor in themselves, throw some light on the finances and administration of the project.

One of those in arrears was A.C. Jeffrey, a trustee. The committee resolved on 1 October 1851 that, in consequence of Messrs Jeffrey and Gill having fallen above six months in arrears and due notice having been sent to each, lot 45 held by Jeffrey and lot 78 held by Gill should be deemed forfeit. It was also resolved that notice be served on five other subscribers, including Doran, a member of the committee, informing them that unless their arrears were paid by the next pay-day, their shares would then be deemed forfeit. Perhaps not surprisingly, this rigorous treatment of himself and less rigorous treatment of others did not please Jeffrey, and in February 1856 the committee was told that Jeffrey was refusing to sign any more conveyances of lots unless he was paid one guinea each time. The committee wrote to Jones, their lawyer, who informed the committee on 19 May that Jeffrey refused to sign any more conveyances unless he was refunded a sum of £50 alleged by him to have been paid into the company and, if this was considered an illegal claim, then he would insist on an indemnity. Jones continued that the chairman, W.W. Smith, had been consulted but had opined that this was not a matter for the company and that shareholders requiring conveyances and objecting to paying a fee for a signature should themselves take legal action against Jeffrey. In the event, the six shareholders involved had preferred to pay the guinea fee rather than sue. The matter appears to have gone unresolved until the death of Jeffrey in September 1859, which left Okell as the sole trustee.

Another dispute involved George Summers, who had become chairman of the company in October 1848. By resolution of the committee on 10 May 1851 the commission for the architectural work on the lodge had been given to Henry Summers. A design was submitted, but at the general meeting of October 1851 it was resolved that the matter should stand adjourned until

November, so that the members could inspect the plans. Only a committee meeting is recorded as being held on the 5 November, and at this it was resolved that the adoption of the present plans for the lodge should be deferred until at least three further plans could be submitted to the members. A further committee meeting was called by George Summers on 7 November so that he could obtain copies of all the minutes and resolutions regarding the lodge: it was resolved that he be allowed only the same facilities to take abstracts as any other member of the company. A general meeting held on 19 December 1851 discussed at length a circular sent to the members by Henry Summers complaining about the committee's reversal of its earlier decision, but a resolution was passed confirming the consideration of three further plans. Two subscribers, Woods and Ireland, tried to save the situation by proposing that Henry Summers' plans be adopted but only two votes were recorded in favour. George Summers, who had 'had to leave' the meeting, resigned as chairman in January 1852. No proof can be offered that George and Henry Summers were related, but if they were, it might explain the former's enthusiasm for the plan submitted. Henry Summers subsequently obtained a county court judgment against the company for £30 15s 0d in respect of the fee for his design.[19]

By the time the project as envisaged by the original promoters was nearing completion, John Jones, the company's lawyer, was falling out of favour with the membership. In 1851, he drew up the conveyance to the trustees, the deed of covenant and the deed of conveyance of the land given for the church. He then offered to do the conveyance from the trustees to individual members for £5 each (without stamps).[20] Later he improved his offer; the cost would now be £4 12s 6d per member. However, at the general meeting of October 1851, the shareholders unanimously resolved that the proprietors should have the option of employing any solicitor to make the conveyance, subject to a charge of one guinea by the company's solicitor, and that the private solicitor should have the privilege of copying the company's draft of the form of conveyance, which was to be adhered to. However, from the attestations on the deed of covenant referred to above, it is evident that Jones continued to hold the deed and act for the trustees, although the committee afterwards employed the firm of Dodge and Wynne on occasions as required, for instance, in the action against Leyland to be discussed shortly.

At the committee meeting of 7 April 1852 it was decided that there should no longer be monthly meetings, but that the chairman - now William Warren Smith, elected to replace George Summers - should call one as required. The next minuted committee meeting is on 20 October 1852, before the general meeting held on that date. In 1853, there were committee meetings on 31 March, 12 May and 16 September, but no general meeting was called. A lengthy agenda was dealt with at a committee meeting on 3 March 1854, prior to a general meeting of 31 March 1854, when the only business dealt with was the disposal of the farmhouse still on the land (it was sold by private 'ticket' to Leyland for £14 12s 7d and was to be pulled down by 1 July). Only one other committee meeting was held in 1854, when the matter of damage to Mr Astley's garden wall revived. The slowing down of committee activity was perhaps not merely because the initial stages of the project were now decided if not wholly completed.

In fact there seems to have been growing discontent with the lack of active management of the estate. A Special General Meeting called by fifteen members holding 34 lots - including some of the members of the committee elected in 1852 - was invited to consider the financial state of the company, the completion of the works, the advisability of disposal of the lots belonging to the company or any other way of raising funds to complete the works, and the propriety of asking the trustees to sanction the appointment of a committee of five to be named at the meeting who 'shall have power to receive the rent of the Lodge, collect arrears and take the general management of the estate during the pleasure of the General body'. Most of this agenda was accepted by the meeting held on 7 December 1854 and five proprietors were elected as a new committee - George Woods, H.G. Ireland, W.W. Smith, William Kershaw and J.A.D. Watts. The real or alleged reasons for this action were later explained in correspondence with William Okell, one of the two trustees, in the course of a dispute with him over the matter of a bill from Jones for services rendered to the trustees. Okell appears to have felt that the new committee was acting in a manner not in accordance with the trust deed. The committee replied as follows:-

> the committee have never arrogated to themselves the power of
> acting without the sanction of the trustees; as they received their

authority from the proprietors at the meeting of 7 December 1854 which was duly sanctioned in writing by both of the trustees: that this committee have been the means of keeping the affairs of the proprietors in order, and rescuing the Estate from the neglected condition in which it was previous to their appointment and they have been duly recognised by every successive annual meeting of proprietors. Further, in the opinion of this committee, the conduct of Mr. Jones in ignoring its existence after having acted under their instruction in preparing conditions of sale and receiving payment from them for same, is offensive to this committee and not justifiable considering his knowledge of all the facts of the case.[21]

It would appear that Jones, like Okell, had reservations about the activities, if not the legality, of the new, smaller committee.

After the dispute with Jeffrey, the other trustee, ended with his death on 27 September 1859, Okell, who had long lived away from Liverpool, indicated that he wished to resign as trustee.[22] At the Annual General Meeting of 2 July 1860, Walter Bostock and William Kershaw were elected trustees to replace Jeffrey and Okell. But at the meeting, Ralph Leyland and John Bennett tried to delay their appointment, on the grounds that, since the notice of the meeting had not mentioned the question of appointment of new trustees, notice should now be given and another meeting held. There were only two votes for this amendment.

Leyland was yet another of the original promoters of the scheme who found himself in dispute with the new order. Three issues arose. First, on 28 May 1855 the committee refused Leyland's request to make temporary use of the sewers to drain his shops on the high road. (A month later, the township surveyor sent in a request to inspect the sewers - the minutes ignore the likely connection.) Secondly, on 6 October 1856 the Committee of Works reported that Leyland's boundary wall did not conform to the trust deed. Leyland was written to and when he failed to reply the chairman was instructed to see Leyland and threaten legal action. Leyland responded that the infringement, if it existed, was unintentional. (Bennett, Leyland's ally in the attempt to delay the appointment of the new trustees, was also causing difficulty at this time by refusing to give up the deeds and books of the company to the new committee, claiming that he held them on behalf of Jeffrey.) The third issue then arose. The Committee of Works reported that there were two houses in separate occupation on plot 24 in contravention of the trust deed.[23] The plot was owned by Leyland and one of the two houses was the farmhouse purchased in March 1854, on the condition that it would be pulled down. Evidently, Leyland had instead let it. On 19 April 1858 the Committee of Works reported that Leyland was resisting the complaint about occupation of the farmhouse and refused to arbitrate, although he had agreed to consider this some months before. At the annual general meeting of 8 July 1858 a resolution was passed authorizing an action against Leyland to enforce the covenants on three points, the farmhouse, the boundary walls of the four houses he had erected, and the lack of palisades on the top of the front walls. The following year it was reported to the annual general meeting that, after commencement of an action, an agreement had been reached whereby Leyland would pull down the farmhouse, lower the boundary walls, and pay the costs of the action, while the committee waived their right to immediate alteration of the rails and coping of the front walls, though taking an acknowledgement from Leyland that they constituted an infringement.

Over the years, gas lamps were added to the roads and seats were placed on the promenade. But the trustees reported to the annual general meeting of July 1867 that the seats had had to be removed, 'as they greatly tended to detain the intruders, who seemed to regard these conveniences to be intended for their accommodation, from the large and un-ceremonious use they made of them'. (The intruders referred to were from Garston Village, 'which has suddenly become a town, crowded with the labouring classes who for some time past have made too free with your private Promenade and property.') At this same general meeting - the last nineteenth-century one fully recorded - there was clearly again some feeling about the way matters were being handled by the committee. Further, there had apparently been a reluctance on the part of members in recent years to pay 'calls' for road maintenance and the like. Occupiers of houses were by covenant responsible for the roads opposite their own lots, but there remained unbuilt plots. At one time general maintenance costs had been met by the 'Grass fund': owners of unbuilt plots were encouraged to permit the trustees to let the grazing of the grass from their lots or to have it cut for sale as hay, the proceeds being used for the repair of the roads opposite the respective lots. The 'Grass fund' account was commenced in May 1856; in 1858 £25 was received from this source. This sum and the rent from the lodge were the only regular sources of income by the 1860s. For a time occasional sums were raised by sale of the lots left in the hands of the company, but by 1866 the trustees proposed, if the proprietors were not prepared to pay calls, to raise money by selling the lodge, the only remaining trust property. This was again proposed in 1867, when a further need for money appeared; it was thought desirable to purchase the manorial rights of the foreshore in anticipation of a proposed dock.[24]. Strains in the administration following the trustees' 1867 report would seem to be revealed by the holding of an Adjourned Extraordinary General Meeting which resolved that 'it would be very unnecessary and inexpedient, and be attended with serious expense, to remove the present trustees and appoint others in their place'.

The years immediately following were much occupied by discussions concerning a proposal to pass a railway through the estate, and by the proposal of the London and North Western Railway Company to build a dock at Garston. While there was hostility to the dock project in the park, there was no willingness to pay for opposing it in Parliament or elsewhere. Allegations were made about the correctness of the Grass Fund accounts and the annual reports of the trustees became somewhat querulous in tone. No annual general meeting was held in 1868, but twelve proprietors convened one by circular in November 1869. The election of a chairman took about fifteen minutes and two rounds of voting, after which William Kershaw took the chair; but some minutes later Ralph Leyland joined the meeting and, having been immediately proposed and seconded, without further ceremony he pushed Kershaw out of the chairman's seat, which Leyland proceeded to occupy under protest from Kershaw (or so it is recorded). Kershaw then read a letter withdrawing his resignation as trustee, after which it was resolved that a vote be taken, presumably to confirm the position of the trustees: Kershaw received forty votes, Halsall thirty-five, and Bostock was opposed by only one vote. (It is difficult to know how to interpret these proceedings so summarily recorded, but it would seem that, as earlier, a clash of personalities enlivened, if it did not necessarily help, the administrative process.) It was next proposed that a call of 10s per lot be made; rival amendments proposed a call of 5s per lot and no call at all. Voting was very close between the 10s call and the nil call and scrutineers were appointed. In the end, it was declared that Kershaw had won: the minutes do not in fact reveal what he had proposed, but it can probably be inferred that as a trustee he had been in favour of the 10s call.

The minute book starts to peter out at this point. There are inconclusive minutes of a general meeting on 6 July 1868, at which a committee of seven was elected to run the estate, and of an annual general meeting on 4 January 1869, with Leyland in the chair, at which the only item of business was the matter of *Bostock and Others v. Huthersall.* Bostock and Kershaw proposed that the appeal to a higher court as advised by the barrister be proceeded with at once. However, an amendment proposed 'that the proceedings in Chancery recently adopted by Messrs. Kershaw and Bostock against Horsfall and Huthersall all having been taken without the consent or sanction of the proprietors and in opposition to the express resolution of the Proprietors Committee, this meeting declines to assume any responsibility for such proceedings'. No indication is given as to which of these resolutions was passed, nor is the cause of the action explained. However, since Huthersall and his wife are recorded in the 1871 census return as a schoolmaster and mistress with six pupils, it is possible that the action against them taken by the trustees was therefore one seeking to prevent them from running a trade or business within the park contrary to the covenants.

Minutes of an annual general meeting on 5 July 1869 are started but the ink appears to have run out after the writer recorded that the accounts had been read and passed. There is then a gap in the records of the company until a new series starts with a record of an Extraordinary General Meeting on 18 February 1878. New trustees were appointed in place of the late Walter Bostock and Thomas Halsall who had left the county, and matters continue as before. The exact significance of the gap in the records is not known, but it may well have been that by 1870, since the teething troubles of the park had been overcome, the management arrangements were so sufficiently settled that the residents displayed less interest in participatory discussions and regular reports.

Forward to the present day

In 1861, there were only eight households in Cressington Park, with 51 residents. But only 15 of these were servants, suggesting that Cressington had lower social status than Grassendale.[25] By 1871, there were 29 inhabited houses and two uninhabited; by 1881, 55 inhabited houses and none uninhabited. Although it had taken some time to become established, by the end of the century the park had become a thriving community. Horse buses had run from Garston to Liverpool for many years, eventually connecting with the electric tramway from Aigburth Vale opened in 1899; a railway line from Garston to Liverpool was built in 1861 and opened in 1864.[26] The railway makes its way through Cressington Park in a cutting, passes outside the gates of Grassendale Park, and tunnels under Fulwood Park. A station was opened in Cressington Park and it is tempting to conclude that this added convenience was the turning point in the expansion of the park.

The name of the park had been originally 'Aigburth Park', as was so resolved at a committee meeting on 5 October 1847. However, at the 1856 annual general meeting it was resolved that it should be renamed 'Cressington Park'. Writing in 1868, a local historian complained that the name Cressington 'had not the slightest topographical value. It is due to an error on the part of an ordnance surveyor and was adopted by gentlemen interested in the property, who appear to have thought that any name would do.'[27] Ordnance Survey maps of the period do note a 'Cressington Farm', although the farm on the site appears to have been known as Grace's Farm (the 1841 tithe map of Garston gave the farm occupier as Thomas Grace). Whatever the justification for the name, the inhabitants of the area took it up and the suburb became known as Cressington, although the church built on the donated plots at the end of the Park on Aigburth Road is still known as St Mary, Grassendale.[28] The area achieved some fame through the 1889 murder trial of Florence Maybrick: she bought some of her poisoned flypapers from Mr Hanson, 'another chemist at Cressington'.[29]

Over the years, the Liverpool park estates have withstood legal challenges; most recently, in 1965 an application to the Lands Tribunal for modification of the covenants on Cressington Park, so that four two-storey terraced houses could be built on three adjoining plots. The application was rejected on the grounds that there had been no change in the character of the neighbourhood or the property since the restrictions were imposed, nor could the applicant demonstrate that the continued existence of the restrictions impeded any reasonable user of the site without securing practical benefits to all users.[30] In evidence, the applicant's surveyor described the mixed style of development of the estate. Building had continued from the 1850s to 1914: very little building took place between 1914 and 1946 but more recently a little infilling had occurred. He described the area generally as good: although at one time the estate had the appearance of going downhill, in the last 10-15 years it had improved and was now a very desirable residential area, 'an entity on its own ... sought after by professional people'. When cross-examined, he admitted that the estate had been scrupulously administered by its trustees for over one hundred years with practically no interference with the restrictive covenants. He could offer only some seven to ten instances of houses on the estate being converted into flats and so being in multiple occupation, out of 107 houses built.

The 1957 Cressington Park case of *Halsall v. Brizell*, which established a principle vital to the survival of such schemes, has already been considered. Reverting to schemes other than in Liverpool, in the Newcastle schemes some if not all of the roads have been adopted, and this may remove the main concern for enforcement of positive covenants. The Park Estate in Nottingham still maintains its own roads and has a committee to oversee such matters but, having been in inception a leasehold scheme, is outside the scope of the present work.[31] The Liverpool schemes have an advantage in being on the river; the roads lead nowhere else and they have therefore not suffered from the pressures which caused difficulty in Victoria Park in Manchester and in Sandfield Park, Liverpool, both of which at one time imposed tolls to try to maintain privacy. Nor have the Parks been 'surroundable' by inferior accommodation. Despite the proximity of a major road, shops and much terraced, semi-detached and Corporation housing, and also Garston dock, and despite the fact that Cressington and Grassendale promenades now adjoin the public promenade and park of Otterspool, these two parks continue to be enclaves of old houses with large gardens, hence properties very attractive to purchasers. All three of the studied Liverpool estate parks are now conservation areas, which may make the covenants redundant, yet there are no signs so far of this being considered to be the case.

The minutes of the Committee of the plot-owners of Cressington Park demonstrate the enormous amount of time and energy which had to be invested in this type of project. Some of the original proprietors may have anticipated a profit: Ralph Leyland in particular, with his shops and at least four houses built in the park and his interest in Grassendale Park as well, may have been one such, yet there must have been easier options for a speculative builder. The saga which the minutes tell is of solid Victorian business and professional men managing their own residential and communal affairs in a way which is coming back into fashion. It would be surprising if present-day Housing Associations, associations of groups of people who chose to build their own homes, are very different from the Victorian associations which created and managed park estates, in respect of the disputes and problems encountered. No doubt residents in such amenity-led communities find themselves divided on issues now, just as they were in the past, but this is unavoidable. As the account above has shown, from the inception of the Liverpool schemes there was occasional ill-feeling and even litigation. But considering that neighbour disputes now form a substantial social and legal problem, the existence of a context in which problems could be resolved, without violence, and in an inexpensive forum, can be reckoned a social gain.

It is notable that the six freehold schemes which have been traced for this study and which have stood the test of time and litigation are all of the deed of mutual covenant type. There has been no landlord, above all no sole landowner, to dictate the form of building, or to consent to variations, or to enforce the covenants. Committees may often produce camels, but the bond of self-interest and self-reliance formed by the type of undertaking discussed in this study has produced something of continuing value to the residents of today. As noted above, the Sheffield freehold land companies were said to have fallen into disrepute because of the profiteering associated with them. Little if any profit factor appears in the Liverpool schemes, and, as we have seen, the residents not uncommonly asserted their will against the original promoters and investors, their concern being that the amenities surrounding their villas, such as the roads, should be adequately maintained; in other words, that the covenants should be observed - though at as little cost as possible to themselves.

There may also be a moral for the future. In the light of the legislation permitting tenants to purchase the freehold of a block of flats from an absentee management company landlord, it will be necessary for tenants' associations to show the same sort of enthusiasm and determination, if their organisation is to prove more participatory than merely letting an agent do all the work and collect the money. Someone has to 'manage' actively, and that is a burdensome job, largely without tangible reward. Yet in the Liverpool parks, generations of residents have found individuals among them to undertake the tasks; for if the hours do not produce the men, presumably schemes collapse, as indeed many have. It is true that some schemes have been rendered unnecessary, or at least less necessary, by the adoption of roads by local authorities, and by the provision of services such as gas, electricity and water from central sources. However, with the privatization of most of the ultilities, there may be additional scope for private, self-help residential schemes.

NOTES TO CHAPTER 7

1.   This chapter is based on the title deeds and other documents produced by and for the Trustees of Cressington Park and at present in the care of their committee. The documents of Cressington Park Committee are hereafter signalled as CPC.

2.   CPC Minutes, 4 January 1848.

3.   R.S. Crook of Liverpool was a member of the Inner Temple and was called in November 1830: *Law List 1840.*

4.   *Gore*, 1839, 54; 1857, 24.

5.   *Gore*, 1837, 405; 1843, 507; 1851 591; 1851 census return.

6.   *Gore*, 1829, 91; 1843, 155.

7.   A document exists for Cressington Park which is not found among the extant documents of the other two estate parks. Known as 'The Book', it seems to be a register of members and was perhaps originally intended to operate in the style of a book kept, for instance, at the Liverpool Athenaeum, which records the transmission of individual shares from member to member. The pages are divided into 174 numbered boxes, the same number as that of the lots. But the numbers correspond in only 49 instances with the plot number signed on the plan, while the names entered are not signatures. Possibly this is the record made of the original lots drawn in the ballot of February 1849, lots which may well have been exchanged or sold before conveyances were taken, since this would explain why not all the names correspond to signatures on the deed of covenant. Yet some names were clearly added much later, for instance, that of The Cheshire Lines Railway Company. (The first mention of a proposal to build a railway through the park was at the committee meeting of 19 December 1858, and the act authorising the line actually to be built was not passed until 1861). St Mary's Church, opened on 14 August 1853 and consecrated 4 July 1854, was also recorded in boxes 40 and 41. The decision to make these lots available for the church, by exchange with other lots (these lots having belonged originally to Abraham Horsfall, whose name can be discerned faintly on these lots on the plan), was not taken until November 1849, nine months after the ballot. A further puzzling feature of this document is that William Kershaw appears as the recorded holder of about a dozen lots; in three instances, a transfer of one of those lots is recorded, but the plan is signed by Kershaw on only one lot. Kershaw became a trustee in 1860 and so company lots or forfeited lots may have been recorded in his name, but there is no mention of his co-trustee, Walter Bostock. It has been suggested that 'The Book' was an attempt to ensure compliance with the covenant scheme by later purchasers, but most of the names are those of signatories of the deed of covenant itself and the attempt does not appear to have been continued to include all future purchasers of lots; except in the three cases mentioned, only one name appears in each box. Altogether, 'The Book' is a puzzle, but the simplest explanation is that it is a mere register of the original members.

8. In the record of the marriage of William Horsfall and Louisa Ellen Bradbury at Bidston on 25 August 1869, the occupation of Abraham Horsfall, William's father, was recorded as that of 'engineer'.

9. *Gore*, 1834, 269.

10. *Gore*, 1827 177.

11. One of Ballantyne's trade assignees objected to the release on the grounds that future liabilities were uncertain. Leyland was deputed to meet the assignee, with an offer to limit the amount payable on Ballantyne's ten shares to £165 per lot. This Leyland did; apparently the offer was accepted but the assignee then went to Holland. Once all the assignees had been satisfied, Ingram and Ballantyne had to sign. It was reported by Jones that Ingram had signed on 6 March 1850 but that Ballantyne refused to do so without the consent of his solicitor. A deputation was sent to threaten him with an application to the Lord Chancellor to compel signing; it reported that Ballantyne would sign for a bond of indemnity and £10.

12. It is not made clear what the purpose of brick-making at an early stage was, but presumably the bricks were to be used for the sea-wall, promenade and sewers.

13. CPC Minutes, 3 August 1847.

14. CPC Minutes, 31 August 1847.

15. CPC Minutes, 30 January 1851.

16. CPC Minutes, 11 September 1851.

17. CPC Minutes, 17 December 1851.

18. The plans and specifications for this building costing under £500 cover some fourteen foolscap pages.

19. CPC Minutes, 12 May 1853.

20. CPC Minutes, 5 February 1851.

21. CPC Minutes, 7 August 1859.

22. Okell appears to have left Liverpool sometime between 1849 (*Gore*, 1849, 431) and signing the deed of covenant on 16 December 1851, when he gave his place of residence as Glasgow.

23. CPC Minutes, 22 June 1857.

24. It is not clear why this was necessary. As stated earlier there is apparently evidence that the strand had been purchased by William Hope before 1792.

25. Admittedly the balance was affected by the household of Alfred Bram, tallow chandler, whose wife, three sons, two daughters and a sister-in-law were supported by only one servant.

26.   J.B. Horne and T.B. Maund, *Liverpool transport vol I 1830-1900* (London, 1975), 112.

27.   Boult, *Aigburth and Garston*, 158.

28.   In the record of William Horsfall's marriage on 25 August 1869 (note 8 above), his residence was given as 'Cressington, Garston'.

29.   The Maybrick house in Riversdale Road was within walking distance of shops at the end of Cressington Park. *The Times* of 4 August printed the evidence of two chemists; Thomas Noakes, chemist in Aigburth Road, said that Mrs Maybrick obtained one dozen flypapers and paid for them despite the deceased having an account there; a few days later Mr Hanson sold her some lotion and two dozen flypapers, which she paid for in cash, although she did not do this usually.

30.   *Re Shaw's Application*, LT/47/1965; (1966) 18 P & CR 144.

31.   M.A. Simpson and T.H. Lloyd, eds, *Middle class housing in Britain* (London, 1977), 153-69.

Past and Future

The social consequences of the post-1700 surge of British population have been commented upon by many writers ever since the phenomenon first became obvious. One feature was the emergence of a vigorous, individualistic urban middle class, a class which soon developed a powerful urge to own the freehold of the family residence and thus shake off the demeaning control of a landlord over their 'home'. This desire merged with what appears to have been a peculiarly English manifestation of the belief in the virtues of rural life - a belief which has increased rather than diminished the further urban man has moved away from his rural roots. The consequence in the nineteenth century was the development of 'leafy suburbs'. It was to these suburbs that the middle class increasingly escaped, leaving behind the enforced and over-intense communality of the inner cities and becoming instead, as it were, monarchs of all they surveyed - more or less. The suburban villa stood for the adage - 'An Englishman's home is his castle'.

This study has examined the rise of park estates, amenity-led and therefore covenanted building schemes. In particular, schemes by mutual covenant have been discussed. All such schemes depend on a balance between utility and inconvenience. If the covenants on which a scheme depends are too restrictive and inconvenient, then either the residents will reach a mutual agreement to ignore them, or litigation, on the grounds that times have changed and the covenants are no longer reasonable or useful, will result in the covenants not being upheld. Prudent residents' associations are therefore obliged to go some way towards accommodating variation on a consensual basis. As a result successful schemes have persisted over the years, bending when times are hard and holding to a stricter line when market forces allow them to. For instance, there have been times when large, old houses were virtually unsaleable save for conversion to perhaps a school or, more recently, a nursing home. In the 1980s, however, interest in returning such properties to use as a family home revived. If house prices remain relatively depressed at the turn of the century, then conversion to flats may be an appropriate commercially-viable use, as it was in the 1950s and 1960s.

Over the years since schemes came to be recognised by the courts, the prevailing judicial wind has blown in different directions, as described in foregoing chapters: first, the use of contractual terms by conveyancers to protect the 'things of delight' which the common law had scorned in the seventeenth century to protect as easements; next, the recognition by the Royal Commissioners that the protection of amenity by this means was a widespread and valuable practice; then, following the recommendations of the Commissioners, the struggle to convince judges and legal writers that such contractual arrangements were of sufficient benefit to occupiers to outweigh the undoubted inconvenience of a potentially perpetual restriction on the freedom of a freeholder. Almost as soon as this last point was achieved, the political need for renewed building activity after the First World War led to the introduction of a mechanism for review and release, or amendment, of obsolete covenants. The 1925 property legislation reflected, apparently, a reluctance on the part of the judiciary to recognise further building schemes. After the Second World War, planning regulation took over many of the functions of the scheme, and hence it was not until the 1970s, with the growth of interest in conservation, that judges became again more willing to recognise the utility of contractually created schemes.

In 1967, the Leasehold Reform Act permitted many tenants of dwelling houses with a leasehold interest of more than 21 years to demand a conveyance of the freehold from their landlord on favourable purchase terms, although this did not apply to flats because of the difficulties in enforcing positive covenants between freeholders, often necessary for proper maintenance of the building. In the last thirty years the several committees appointed to consider reform of the law in this area have generally recommended a change in the law to make the benefit of both positive and restrictive covenants as enforceable between freeholders as they are between landlord and tenant. However, despite the fact that several acts have been introduced to reform the law on leaseholds by encouraging landlords to hand freehold interests over to their tenants, no legislation has so far been introduced to effect enforceable covenants between freeholders. The Leasehold Reform Housing and Urban Development Act of 1993 failed to address the fundamental point that there is no simple method of enforcing maintenance covenants if flats are sold freehold. Consequently it will still be necessary to employ legal devices such as the creation of a limited company in which residents are the shareholders to achieve either control by tenants of their own building, or the enforceability of positive covenants for the preservation of amenity (such as fencing and maintenance of open space) between the owners of freehold houses.

Ultimately how schemes will fare in the future depends on what Parliament enacts. Modern governments seem to pay little attention to the lawyers appointed to advise them on orderly reform of the law, and at present the technical reform of property law is attracting little interest amid the welter of more pressing political issues. Left to itself, the common law develops by an evolutionary process, as it attempts to meet and balance conflicting interests in the context of the prevailing social, political and economic constraints. At base level, individual lawyers endeavouring to satisfy the demands of clients can only mould the law as it stands within the ideological parameters of the times in which they are operating.

In conclusion, old and new building schemes continue to operate wherever residents are sufficiently concerned about their surroundings to support and participate in the necessary management structures. They are required to demonstrate that concern in the face of regular challenge by developers and by new owners of property within the area of the scheme. To date, with a measure of legal as well as popular support, the schemes are holding their own.

APPENDIX

FULWOOD PARK

ARTICLES OF AGREEMENT REGULATING THE USE HOLDING AND
ENJOYMENT OF LANDS IN TOXTETH PARK THE PROPERTY OF MESSRS.
SMITH

THIS INDENTURE made the Twenty Seventh day of October in the year of our Lord
1840 between WILLIAM SMITH and ALEXANDER SMITH the Younger both of
Liverpool in the County of Lancaster merchants of the first part the several other
persons whose names are hereunto subscribed and seals affixed (except Charles
Stewart Parker, merchant, and Thomas Forsyth, Broker, both of Liverpool aforesaid)
of the second part and the said CHARLES STEWART PARKER and THOMAS
FORSYTH of the third part WHEREAS the said William Smith and Alexander Smith
are seized of or well entitled to certain Pieces or Parcels of Land situate in Toxteth
Park in the said County of Lancaster which are particularly delineated in the Map or
Plan thereof drawn upon or annexed to these presents for an Estate of Inheritance in
fee simple in possession
    AND WHEREAS the said William Smith and Alexander Smith have laid out
part of the said Pieces or Parcels of Land for building purposes in lots as shown in
the said Plan and intend to lay out and allot and offer for sale the remainder of the
said land for similar purposes
    AND WHEREAS for the purpose of insuring to persons who shall become
purchasers of the said Pieces or Parcels of Land the convenient and beneficial holding
and enjoyment of such parts as they respectively purchase and of certain easements
and privileges as connected with the same the said William Smith and Alexander
Smith have proposed and agreed that they and all persons who shall become
purchasers as aforesaid shall enter into such covenants and agreements on their
respective parts as are hereinafter contained
    NOW THIS INDENTURE WITNESSETH that for the purposes aforesaid and
in consideration of the covenants and agreements hereinafter contained on the part of
the said parties hereto of the second part they the said William Smith and Alexander
Smith do hereby for themselves jointly and severally and for their joint and several
Heirs Executors and Administrators covenant promise and agree with and to the said
Charles Stewart Parker and Thomas Forsyth their Executors and Administrators and
also as a separate covenant with and to the said parties hereto of the third part and
their respective Heirs Executors and Administrators and also as a separate covenant
with and to the person and persons who shall from time to time be appointed Trustees
and Trustee under these presents under the power for that purpose hereinafter
contained their and his respective Executors and Administrators in manner and form

following that is to say

THAT they the said William Smith and Alexander Smith their Heirs or assigns shall and will at their own expense within five years of the date hereof open and complete in good and effectual manner and to the satisfaction of the said Charles Stewart Parker and Thomas Forsyth their Executors or Administrators or other the Trustees or Trustee for the time being of these presents the whole of a road to lead from the Park Road to the shore of the River Mersey through their said lands and also shall and will within the same period and in the like manner make and complete the foot-walks on each side of the same road and put up a gate at the entrance of the said road from the Park Road

THAT the said road from the Park Road to the point B with the foot-walks and gate shall be opened made and completed within twelve months from the date hereof as the same is delineated on the said Plan and within the like period a cart-road to the satisfaction of the said Charles Stewart Parker and Thomas Forsyth shall be continued by the said William Smith and Alexander Smith from the said point B to the River Mersey and within five years from the date hereof the remainder of the said road and foot-walks from the said point B to the River Mersey shall be completed AND ALSO that they the said William Smith and Alexander Smith or their Heirs shall and will at their own expence keep and maintain the respective parts of the said road and foot-walks and gate in good repair and condition for the period of twelve months after the said Charles Stewart Parker and Thomas Forsyth or the survivor of them his Executors and Administrators or others the Trustees or Trustee for the time being of these presents shall by writing under their or his hands or hand have certified that the same have been completed as a permanent road to their or his satisfaction AND ALSO that the same roads when opened and completed shall from time to time and at all times thereafter remain and be a carriage and foot-road for the exclusive use and enjoyment of the owners for the time being of the land shown on the said plan AND ALSO that they the said William Smith and Alexander Smith their Heirs or Assigns shall and will within twelve months from the date hereof make and complete in a good and effectual manner and to the satisfaction of Charles Stewart Parker and Thomas Forsyth or the survivor of them his Executors or Administrators or other the Trustees or Trustee for the time being of these presents a main sewer to commence at the point A shown on the said plan and to communicate with the River Mersey and that the said main sewer when made and completed shall from time to time and at all times thereafter remain and be for the exclusive use of the owners for the time being of the lots delineated in the said plan and numbered from 7 to 30 both inclusive AND ALSO that the said William Smith and Alexander Smith their Heirs or Assigns shall not nor will at any time hereafter either wholly or partially make or burn any bricks on any part of the land lying at a greater distance than one hundred and thirty yards from the River Mersey and shall not nor will after the thirty-first day of December One Thousand Eight Hundred and Forty either wholly or partially make or burn any bricks on any part of the said land shown on the said plan except for the purpose of being used or sold for buildings or other erections on the said land.

AND ALSO that they the said William Smith and Alexander Smith their Heirs or Assigns shall not nor will make any alteration or variation in any respect from the said plan as regards lots 9, 11, 17, and 19, and shall not nor will sell or convey any other part of the said land shown on the said plan in lots containing a less quantity than one statute acre without the consent of a general or special meeting of the owners for the time being of land therein delineated to be held as hereinafter mentioned AND ALSO that they the said William Smith and Alexander Smith their Heirs and Assigns shall and will in every contract which they shall hereafter enter into for the sale of any part of the said land insert a stipulation that the person or persons with whom they shall so contract shall enter into and execute these presents AND ALSO that they the said William Smith and Alexander Smith their Heirs and Assigns in respect of the land shown on the said plan which shall from time to time remain unsold and unconveyed AND ALSO as to such part or parts of the said land as shall have been sold and conveyed whereof the purchaser or respective purchasers whereof shall not have executed these presents shall and will observe perform fulfil and keep the several covenants stipulations and agreements hereinafter contained and which on the part of the purchasers of the said land are to be observed performed fulfilled and kept and except the stipulation as to the making of bricks AND ALSO save and except the stipulation rendering it incumbent on each of the said purchasers to erect a Dwelling-house on the land purchased by them respectively PROVIDED NEVERTHELESS that in case the said William Smith and Alexander Smith their Heirs or Assigns shall elect to erect any Messuages Dwelling-houses and Outbuildings on any part of the said land each such Dwelling-house and Outbuildings shall be erected in the manner and subject to the stipulations hereinafter contained.

AND each of the said parties hereto of the third part doth hereby for Himself and Herself his and her respective Heirs Executors Administrators and Assigns acts deeds and defaults only and as to for and concerning the part and parts of the said land which shall have been conveyed to him or her covenant promise and agree with and to the said Charles Stewart Parker and Thomas Forsyth their Executors and Administrators - and also as a separate covenant with and to the person and persons who shall from time to time be appointed Trustees or Trustee of these presents under the power for that purpose hereinafter contained their and his respective Executors and Administrators that they the said parties hereto of the second part respectively and their respective Heirs and Assigns shall and will from time to time and at all times hereafter observe perform fulfil and keep all and every the stipulations and agreements hereinafter contained or such and so many of the same stipulations and agreements respectively as relate to the lands which have been conveyed to them respectively that is to say

THAT no bricks shall be made or burnt either wholly or partially on any part of the said land

THAT the purchaser of each lot of the said land his or her heirs or assigns shall and will expend the sum of one thousand five hundred pounds at least in the erection of a Dwelling-house with suitable outbuildings and conveniences thereon and in fencing and laying out the said Land and shall not erect more than one such Dwelling-house on each statute acre of the said land without the consent of the Majority of the owners for the time being of the other land shown on the said plan

THAT every Dwelling-house which shall hereafter be erected or built shall be erected or built of stone or of brick cemented stuccoed or rough cast and shall not be higher than two stories above the ground exclusive of basement and of attics which attics are to be lighted from the roof.

THAT no Dwelling-house shall be erected on any one of the lots numbered 9, 11, 13, 15, 17, 19 nearer to the road leading from the Park road to the River Mersey than forty feet nor shall any such Dwelling-House extend further therefrom than one hundred and five feet nor nearer either the eastern or western side of any of the said lots than thirty feet and no stables or other outbuildings shall be erected on any one of the said lots nearer the before mentioned road than twenty yards nor extend further therefrom than thirty five yards.

THAT the site of the Dwelling-house and outbuildings to be erected on any other part of the said land than on the lots last mentioned shall be approved by the architects for the time being of the said William Smith and Alexander Smith their heirs or assigns before the erection of the same.

THAT no Dwelling-house to be erected on any part of the said land shall be let or used for any other purpose than a private Dwelling-house and not as a lodging-house or boarding-school without the consent in writing of the majority of owners for the time being of the other land shown on the said plan and if such consent shall be given in any one instance the same shall not operate or be considered as an implied consent in any other instance.

THAT the boundary walls next the said road leading from the Park-road to the River Mersey and the Railing on the top thereof shall be of a uniform height and no boundary division or party wall or fence shall be built on any part of the said land exceeding five feet in height exclusive of the railing or hedge on the top thereof except the garden walls which shall not exceed twelve feet in height and no close boarding shall be used to prevent persons from seeing through any railings or fences.

THAT the said road foot paths and gate hereinbefore covenanted to be made and completed by the said William Smith and Alexander Smith their Executors Administrators or Assigns shall from time to time and at all times after the expiration of the period of twelve months from the respective times the same shall have been completed to the satisfaction of the said Charles Stewart Parker and Thomas Forsyth their Executors or Administrators or other the Trustees or Trustee for the time being of these presents as hereinbefore mentioned to be kept in good and effectual repair at the expenses of the owners for the time being of the land shewn on the said plan who shall pay and contribute towards such costs and charges in the proportions following that is to say each owner shall pay and contribute towards such expenses in the proportions that the number of superficial square yards of the said plan of which he shall for the time being be such owner bears to the whole number of superficial square yards contained in the land shewn on the said plan.

THAT the person or persons purchasing any of the lots shewn on the said plan except the lots 1 to 6 inclusive shall contribute towards the expences of making and completing the main sewer hereinbefore covenanted to be made and completed by the said William Smith and Alexander Smith their heirs or assigns in the proportions following that is to say each purchaser of the respective lots and of any part of the said land shall contribute towards such expence in the proportion that the number of superficial square yards of each of the said lots or of such part of the said land of which he shall for the time being be owner bears to the whole number of superficial square yards contained in the said lots and land the sum of one penny per superficial square yard to be paid by him on his executing these presents and the remainder of the cost thereof immediately after the said sewer shall be made and completed to the satisfaction of the said Charles Stewart Parker and Thomas Forsyth their Executors or Administrators as hereinbefore mentioned.

THE said main sewer shall from time to time and at all times after the same shall have been made and completed to the satisfaction of the said Charles Stewart Parker and Thomas Forsyth their Executors or Administrators or other the Trustees or Trustee for the time being of these presents be kept and maintained in good and substantial repair by the owners for the time being of the said lots numbered 7 to 21 and by the owners of the land lying between those lots and the River Mersey who shall contribute towards such expence in like proportion as they are by the stipulations lastly hereinbefore contained to contribute to the expences of making and completing the said sewer.

THE said Charles Stewart Parker and Thomas Forsyth their Executors or Administrators or other the Trustees or Trustee for the time being of these presents shall from time to time have and may exercise the same powers and remedies for recovering from the owners or occupiers of any of the said land shewn on the said plan the proportion of the expence of keeping and maintaining the said road gate and main sewer in repair which shall from time to time be due from such owners respectively as they would have had and might have exercised if they or he the said Charles Stewart Parker and Thomas Forsyth their Executors or Administrators or the said Trustees or Trustee for the time being had been seized of the land in respect whereof such proportion shall be so due and the same had been due to them or him from the owner or occupier of the said land as rent reserved in respect thereof.

THAT a general meeting of the owners for the time being of land shown on the said plan shall be held on the first Tuesday in January in every year subsequent to the date thereof at such place as may be from time to time agreed upon for the purpose of considering and determining what sum or sums of money shall be contributed and paid by the said owners for the time being of the said land to defray the expences of keeping in repair the said road and main sewer and gate and for the purpose of making all such orders and directions in pursuance of and consistent with the provisions hereinbefore contained as may be thought expedient and determined upon in regard to the common interest of the owners for the time being of the said land.

AND ALSO that the owners for the time being of the larger part of the said land may from time to time call a special general meeting of the other owners for the time being of the said land to consider and determine upon all or any of the matters and things aforesaid fourteen days previous notice of every such general or special meeting being delivered at or sent by post to the last known place of abode or business of such owners and every question to be decided at such annual or general meeting shall be decided by a majority of the owners present in person or by proxy in writing at such meeting each owner to have one vote in right of each entire quantity of one thousand yards of land held by him (subject nevertheless as regards the said William Smith and Alexander Smith theirs Heirs and Devisees to the provision hereinafter contained) and in case of equality of votes or any other matter than the appointment of a Chairman such Chairman shall have a casting vote in addition to his ordinary vote.

THAT the decision of such Meeting as aforesaid shall be binding upon every owner for the time being of the said land notwithstanding any one or more of such owners may not be justified to vote or may be under any personal disability whatsoever and every such Annual Meeting shall have power to appoint one or more committee or committees and also a treasurer from among the owners for the time being of the said land for the ensuing year and such committee or committees shall have all such power and authorities as the said Annual Meeting may think fit to delegate and that the treasurer for the time being shall act as the agent of the said Trustees or Trustee for the time being to receive all sums of money which shall become payable in pursuance of the provisions in these presents contained and to pay and apply the same according to the stipulations regulations and agreements herein contained.

PROVIDED ALWAYS THAT the whole number of votes which the said William Smith and Alexander Smith and any person claiming through them as Heirs or Devisees shall be entitled to give at any such meeting as aforesaid in respect of such land as shall for the time being remain unsold shall not at any time exceed one-third of the whole number of votes which the persons who shall have become purchasers of any part of the said land their Heirs or Assigns would be entitled to give if present at any such Meeting.

PROVIDED ALWAYS THAT no resolution authorising the sale of any part of the said land in lots containing a less quantity than one acre or dispensing with any of the restrictions contained in these presents applicable to such lots shall be proposed at any general or special Meeting unless notice in writing of the intention to propose such resolution be delivered at or sent by post to the last known place of abode or business of each of the owners of land shewn in the said plan.

AND IT IS HEREBY AGREED AND DECLARED that if the said Charles Stewart Parker and Thomas Forsyth or either of them their or either of their Executors or Administrators or any Trustees or Trustee to be appointed as hereinafter mentioned shall die or desire to be discharged from or refuse or decline or become incapable to act in the trusts hereby reposed in them or him as aforesaid then and so often as the same shall happen it shall be lawful for any Annual or other General Meeting of the owners for the time being of the land shewn on the said plan to nominate substitute or appoint any other person or persons to be a trustee or trustees in the place of the trustee or trustees so dying desiring to be discharged from or refusing declining or becoming incapable to act as aforesaid and every trustee to be appointed as aforesaid shall have and may exercise all the same powers as if he had been herein named and appointed and the several Covenants hereinbefore contained had been entered into with him.

AND IT IS HEREBY FURTHER AGREED that any and every resolution made at such Annual or General Meeting as aforesaid nominating and appointing any future trustees or trustee shall be conclusive evidence against all the said parties hereto of the second part and their respective heirs and assigns and every of them and against all persons claiming under them that such appointment was legally and duly made.

PROVIDED ALWAYS AND IT IS HEREBY AGREED AND DECLARED between the parties to these presents that if the said William Smith and Alexander

Smith their heirs or assigns shall at any time hereafter open or make any entrance from certain land of or to which he or they are now seized or entitled lying to the westward of and adjoining to the land shewn on the said plan into the said Road to be made by the said William Smith and Alexander Smith their heirs or assigns and shall themselves enter or procure the person to whom they shall sell the land so communicating with the said Road to enter into Covenants with the said Charles Stewart Parker and Thomas Forsyth their executors or administrators or other the trustees or trustee for the time being similar to the Covenants hereinbefore contained for contributing towards the expences of keeping the said Road in repair in the proportion that the whole number of superficial square yards of such land bears to the whole number of superficial square yards of land for the time being contributing towards such expence and shall grant to them or him the same powers and remedies for recovering such proportion then the owner or owners for the time being of the said land shall and may use and enjoy the said Road in common with the owners for the time being of the land shewn in the said plan.

AND IT IS HEREBY AGREED AND DECLARED between and by the parties to these presents of the first and second parts that it shall and may be lawful for them or any of them or any persons claiming through them or any of them to apply for and obtain the aid of a Court of Equity for compelling the specific performance and restraining by injunction the breach of any of the clauses stipulations and agreements herein contained by the other or others of them or any person or persons claiming through the other or others of them IN WITNESS whereof the said parties to these presents have hereunto set their hands and seals the day and year first before written.

PARTIES	WITNESSES
William John Tomlinson	Charles F. Cameron
Thos.Avison	Charles F. Cameron
W.H. Goore	Thomas Rigge
Joseph Miller	William Myers Jr.
Hugh McNeile	Ambrose Lace
J.P. Younghusband	Ambrose Lace
John Eden	Edward Hy. Roscoe
Geo.B. Carter	Edward Hy. Roscoe
William Bower	Edward Hy. Roscoe
T.B. Forwood	Edward Hy. Roscoe
Chas. Cotesworth	Edward Hy. Roscoe
Robert Wynne	Edward Hy. Roscoe
J. Yate Lee	Edward Hy. Roscoe

James Birkett   Edward Hy. Roscoe
Samuel Holme   Hy. Ward Collins
James Holme   Hy. Ward Collins
                          Will Smith
                        Alexr. Smith Jnr.

GRASSENDALE PARK

ABSTRACT OF THE COVENANTS

entered into by the Shareholders of the Aigburth Land Company by Deed of Covenant dated the 9th day of May 1848 as to Building etc. also mode of enforcing annual rate and as to meetings of Shareholders Voting etc.

9th May 1848

BY DEED OF COVENANT of this date made between the several persons whose names and seals were thereunto subscribed and affixed except James Rowan Ralph Leyland William Valiant Willis and John Starr de Wolf of the first part James Dawson Rodick of the second part and the said James Rowan Ralph Leyland William Valiant Willis and John Starr de Wolf of the third part the parties thereto respectively covenanted as follows:-

THE parties thereto of the first part covenanted with the said James Dawson Rodick and as a separate covenant with the said James Rowan Ralph Leyland William Valiant Willis and John Starr de Wolf as follows:-

FIRST- That not more than one dwelling-house should be erected on each or any one of the said plots of land and that each such dwelling-house should be of not less value than £400 exclusive of the fences and outbuildings belonging thereto

SECONDLY - That each and every such dwelling-house with every outbuilding should be built of well faced stone or of brick and if of brick should be cemented outside and should not be higher than two stories or thirty feet from the level of the road opposite and should be placed ten yards neither more nor less back from the road including projections except those on the parade which should be placed eight yards back including projections

THIRDLY - That no stable or other outbuilding should be nearer than ten yards from the road boundary walls and that the iron railings fronting the roads together with the front partition walls or boundary separating each lot should be of one uniform height and design and that no temporary fence should be made but such as would be approved of by the said persons parties thereto of the third part

FOURTHLY - That no mill steam engine brewery chemical work lime kiln glass work or slaughter house should be erected on any part of any of the said plots or parcels of land

FIFTHLY - That there should never at any time be carried on upon any of the said several plots of land or upon any part thereof respectively or in any building erected or to be erected upon any of the said plots of land any of the trades manufactures or businesses following this is to say:- Soap Boiler Candle Maker

Skinner or Tanner Brewer Manufacturer of Acids or Alkalies Retailer of Malt or Spirituous Liquors or any other trade manufacture or business whatsoever

SIXTHLY - That in case any building should be erected or begun to be erected on any part of any of the said several plots of land marked with the name of any of the said persons parties hereto of the first part contrary to the stipulations and agreements thereinbefore contained then and in any and every such case and when and so often as the same should happen it should be lawful for the said James Dawson Rodick his heirs and assigns or for the said James Rowan Ralph Leyland William Valiant Willis and John Starr de Wolf or the survivors or survivor of them their or his heirs or assigns or other the Trustees or Trustee for the time being under these presents to enter into and upon any and each parcel of land whereon any such building should be erected or be begun or be in the course of erection respectively and to abate and pull down every such building or by Bill in equity to enjoin or restrain the erection thereof and that in case any building should be erected or be begun to be erected on any part of any of the several plots of land marked with the name of any of the said persons parties hereto of the third part contrary to the stipulations and agreements hereinbefore contained then and in any and every such case and when and so often as the same should happen it should be lawful for the others or other of them the said persons parties thereto of the third part or the survivors or survivor of such other his heirs or other Trustee or Trustees for the time being to enter into and upon any and each plot of land whereon any such building should be erected or be begun of or be in the course of erection respectively and to abate and pull down any such building or by Bill in equity to enjoin or restrain the erection

SEVENTHLY - That each and every of them the said persons parties thereto of the first and third parts respectively and his respective heirs executors administrators and assigns should from time to time contribute and pay a due and just proportion in respect of the plot or several plots of land in the said plan marked with his name respectively and of the dwelling-house on each such plot erected or to be erected in common with the owners of the several other plots of land described in the said plan of all costs charges and expenses which had already been incurred and which should from time to time and at all times thereafter be incurred in or about the forming and constructing and the maintaining and keeping in good repair and cleansing and scouring as well of the several roads or ways described in the said plan and of the Sea Wall and Terrace as also all and every the main drains and main sewers already made or thereafter to be made in or upon any part or parts of the land described in the said plan for the common use convenience and advantage of the owners for the time being of the said several plots of land described in the same plan and of the dwelling-houses erected or to be erected thereon respectively or for the general and common drainage of the same lands and that the expense of lighting the said roads or ways with gas should be contributed and paid by the owners of such dwelling-houses as for the time being should be erected on the said plots of land in equal shares and proportions and that for such respective proportionate share of all such costs charges and expenses as aforesaid of any of the said persons parties thereto of the first part or his or their respective heirs or assigns or the owner or owners for the time being of any of the said plots of land inscribed on the said plan with the name or names of any of the said persons parties thereto of the first part or of the dwelling-house or dwelling-houses thereon erected who should refuse or neglect to pay such proportionate share of such costs charges and expenses the said James Rowan Ralph Leyland William Valiant Willis and John Starr de Wolf or the survivors or survivor of them or their or his heirs executors administrators or assigns or other the Trustees or Trustee for the time being under those presents should when and so often as such refusal or neglect should happen have full power to distrain upon the plot of land messuage or dwelling-house or several and respective plots of land messuages or dwelling-houses the owner or respective owners whereof respectively should have made such neglect in the same manner as landlords were authorised to do for rent in arrear and dispose of such distress or distresses accordingly and that for such respective proportionate share of all such costs charges and expenses as aforesaid of any of the said persons parties thereto of the third part or his or their respective heirs or assigns or the owner or owners for the time being of any of the said plots of land inscribed in the said plan with the name or names of any of the said persons parties thereto of the third part or of the dwelling-house or dwelling-houses thereon erected who should refuse or neglect to pay such proportionate part of such costs charges and expenses the others of them or the survivors or survivor of the others of them the said persons parties thereto of the third part or the executors or administrators of such survivors or other the Trustees or Trustee for the time being should when and so often as such refusal or neglect should happen have full power to distrain upon and should and might distrain upon the plot of land messuage or dwelling-house or several and respective plots of land messuages or dwelling-houses the owner or respective owners whereof respectively should have made such neglect or refusal in the same manner as landlords were authorised to do for rent in arrear and dispose of such distress or distresses accordingly

AND LASTLY - That the several and respective persons parties thereto of the first and third parts respectively and their respective heirs and assigns and the respective owners for the time being of the said several and respective plots of land inscribed in the said plan with the names of the said parties thereto of the first and third parts respectively and of the several and respective dwelling-houses erected or to be erected thereon respectively would from time to time and at all times thereafter abide by and submit to and observe all such lawful and reasonable rules and regulations as should from time to time be made by or on the part of the owners for the time being of the same several plots of land at any meeting to be held as thereafter mentioned for or in relation to the promoting of the better and more convenient and advantageous enjoyment of the whole of the same plots of land and the dwelling-houses thereon or for or in relation to the contribution by the owner or owners for the time being of each of the same plots of land of the means necessary towards the expenses of keeping in repair the said roads sea wall terrace and main drains and sewers and of lighting the said roads with gas

AND the said James Rowan Ralph Leyland William Valiant Willis and John Starr de Wolf did thereby for themselves their heirs executors and administrators covenant with each of the said persons parties thereto of the first part and with his respective heirs executors administrators and assigns that they the said James Rowan Ralph Leyland William Valiant Willis and John Starr de Wolf their heirs and assigns would stand and be seized of and interested in all the roads described in the said plan and thereon coloured yellow and of the terrace and all rights of strand and shore opposite thereto when the same should have been conveyed to and vested in them Upon trust to permit and suffer the same at all times for ever thereafter to be left open and unbuilt upon and to be freely used and enjoyed by the several and respective persons parties thereto of the first and third parts respectively and by their several and respective heirs and assigns and by the owners and occupiers for the time being of the said several and respective plots of land Numbered from 1 to 85 inclusively upon the said plan and of the several and respective dwelling-houses erected and to be erected thereon respectively

AND IT WAS THEREBY AGREED AND DECLARED between and by the said parties thereto of the first and third parts respectively that in the meantime and until the said roads terrace and rights of strand and shore should have been conveyed to the said James Rowan Ralph Leyland William Valiant Willis and John Starr de Wolf their heirs and assigns Upon trust as aforesaid the same roads terrace rights of strand and shore should so far as the same persons parties thereto of the first and third parts respectively and their several and respective heirs and assigns were interested thereon respectively be left open and unbuilt upon and be freely used and enjoyed by the said several persons parties thereto of the first and third parts respectively and by their respective heirs and assigns and by such occupiers as aforesaid

AND for the purpose of agreeing and determining upon the expenses to be from time to time incurred in keeping the said roads terrace and sea wall sewers and lodge in repair and for lighting the said roads with gas and also for making and determining upon the said rules and regulations to be observed for the better more convenient and more advantageous enjoyment of the said several plots of land and the dwelling-houses erected and to be erected thereon and for securing all other objects of those presents it was thereby agreed and declared between the said parties thereto of the first and third parts as follows (that was to say):-

THAT there should be two General Meetings of the proprietors for the time being of the said plots of land and dwelling-houses in every year and to be held on the first Monday in March and the first Monday in September at the Clarendon Rooms in South John Street in Liverpool or at such other place in Liverpool or Aigburth as might from time to time be agreed upon at any meeting or otherwise And an Extraordinary Meeting might also be held at any time when and so often as the Trustees for the time being of the said roads or the proprietors for the time being of twenty or more of the said plots of land should convene the same

THAT of every meeting General or Extraordinary seven clear days' notice in writing specifying the time and place of the meeting and as to every Extraordinary Meeting specifying also the business for which the same was convened should be sent by post or otherwise to the proprietors of the said several plots of land

THAT the presence of ten or more persons being proprietors of twenty or more of the said plots of land should be necessary to constitute any meeting and unless the requisite number attend within one hour after the time appointed and also remain until the business of the meeting be disposed of such meeting should be dissolved

THAT every meeting should in the first place choose a Chairman from among themselves and every proprietor present in person or by proxy (such proxy being a proprietor) should be entitled to vote as follows namely:- The owner of one plot one vote the owner of two and under six plots two votes the owner of six plots and under ten plots three votes the owner of ten plots and upwards four votes But if two or more persons should happen to be owners as joint tenants or tenants in common of any one of the said plots of land they should only have one vote among them in respect of the same respective plots of land and all questions should be determined by a majority of votes the Chairman to have a casting vote besides his own private vote in case of an equality

THAT the determination or resolution of every such meeting should be binding on all the said persons parties thereto of the first and third parts and their respective heirs and assigns But that no expenses for repairs or otherwise should be incurred except such as should be sanctioned by some General or Extraordinary Meeting unless accident should occur as the bursting of a sewer or any destruction by storm or otherwise of the sea wall requiring immediate repair

THAT no rule regulation resolution or determination of any meeting should be annulled or altered but by the determination of two successive subsequent General Meetings

THAT the Trustees for the time being should cause a book to be kept in which the proceedings of every meeting should be entered and the entry of such proceedings of every meeting should be signed by the Chairman thereof and that any General Meeting should have power from time to time (notice having been given in the summons convening the meeting) to remove any person or persons from being a Trustee or Trustees of the said roads sewers terrace wall shore rights lodge and land and to appoint another or others in his or their stead

AND it was thereby further agreed and declared between and by the said persons parties thereto of the first and third parts that the said James Rowan Ralph Leyland William Valiant Willis and John Starr de Wolf their heirs and assigns should stand seized of and interested in the said plot or plots of the said land which should not be allotted to or taken by any of the said persons parties thereto of the first and third parts And also of the said Lodge Upon trust to permit and suffer the said lodge to be used and occupied and enjoyed in such manner as the Trustees for the time being subject to the control of any such meeting or meetings as aforesaid should determine or direct and as to the said last mentioned plot or plots of land and (if any meeting should so direct) also as to the said Lodge Upon trust that they the said Trustees for the time being should sell and absolutely dispose of the same respectively by public auction or private contract subject to all such covenants conditions and restrictions as were thereinbefore expressed and contained concerning the other of the said plots of land which had been taken by the said persons parties thereto of the first and third parts respectively for the best price or prices in money that could reasonably be obtained for the same with liberty to buy in at any auction or auctions and to rescind or vary the terms of any contract for sale and to re-sell by either of the modes aforesaid without being responsible for any loss or expense occasioned thereby and should receive the monies to arise by such sale or sales and give a receipt or receipts for the same which receipt or receipts should effectively exonerate the purchaser or purchasers his her or their heirs and assigns from all responsibility as to the application of the money therein expressed to have been received and from all obligation to enquire as to the propriety of the sale or as to the regularity or propriety of the appointment of any new Trustee or Trustees of the premises if any such appointment should have been made and should apply the moneys arising by such sale or sales after defraying thereout all expenses incident thereto in satisfaction in the first place so far as might be necessary of the original purchase money for the said land and then towards the expenses of making and maintaining in repair the said roads sewers terrace and sea wall and if there should be any surplus then should pay the same between and to the said persons parties of the first and third parts respectively according to their respective shares thereof

AND it was thereby lastly agreed and declared that when and so often as any vacancy should happen in the number of the Trustees of the said roads sewers terrace sea wall lodge land and premises by the death resignation or removal of any of the Trustees for the time being it should be lawful for any meeting convened as aforesaid of the proprietors for the time being of the said plots of land allotted to and taken up by the said persons parties thereto of the first and third parts to appoint a new Trustee to supply and fill up every such vacancy and thereupon the said roads sewers terrace sea wall lodge and premises should from time to time be conveyed so that the same might be vested in the continuing Trustees and such new Trustee jointly Upon the trusts thereinbefore declared and contained or such of them as should be subsisting and capable of taking effect and every new Trustee should have and might exercise and execute in conjunction with his Co-trustees all the powers and authorities thereinbefore contained or such of them as should be subsisting and capable of taking effect.

Notes

The 'parties of the first part' were the fifty-four plot purchasers who signed this deed: James Dawson was the mortgagee and the parties of the third part were the promoters who also purchased plots.

CRESSINGTON PARK

ABSTRACT OF THE DEED OF COVENANT
entered into by the Shareholders of the Second Aigburth Land Company dated 18th
August 1851.

INDENTURE of this date made bwn the several persons whose names and seals are
thrunto subscribed and affixed (except the said Wm.Okell and Alexander Colquhoun
Jeffrey) of the 1st pt and the said Wm Okell and Alexander Colquhoun Jeffrey of the
2nd part

    RECITING the bfre abstracted Indre of the 3rd May 1851 and as thrin was
recited

    AND RECITING that the sd fields or closes of land were purchased by the sd
Wm Okell & Alexander Colquhoun Jeffrey for the ppse of laying out and dividing the
same into the several plots or allotments and forming the ways or roads sea wall and
promenade or otherwise in the manner descd in the plan drawn upon those presents
with a view to the erection of a dwghse with suitable out offices on each of the sd
plots of land as trustees for the sevl and respive persons parties thrto to each of whom
the sevl and respive plot or plots of the sd land in the sd plan inscribed with his
respive name has or had been sevly conveyed as they did thrby resply acknowledge

    AND RECITING that in the Conveyance of each and every of the plots of land
to the sd persons parties thrto were contd on the pt of the Grantees thrby resply
named and their repive heirs exors admors and assns COVENANTS similar in terms
or in effect to the covnts thrinar contd.

    AND RECITING that it had been deemed expedient that three of the sd plots
of land shld be given for the ppse of building a place of Worship of the Established
Church of England

    AND RECITING that the site of the roads and of the sea wall and promenades
descd in the sd plan and thrin for distinction coloured yellow and also the Lodge were
intended to be left vested in the sd Wm Okell and Alexander Colquhoun Jeffrey their
heirs and assns by virtue of the sd last abstracted Conveyance of the 3rd May 1851
UPON TRUST to permit and suffer the same at all times for ever to be freely used
and enjoyed by the sevl persons parties thrto and their respive heirs and assns and by
the occupiers for the time being of the sd sevl plots of land inscribed in the sd plan
with the names of the sd persons parties thrto and of the sevl dwghses erected or to
be erected thron resply and as to such plot or plots of land as shld not be allotted to
or taken by any of the sd persons parties thrto UPON THE TRUSTS thrinar declared

    AND RECITING for better securing the performance of the covnts contd in the
sevl and respive Conveyances of the sevl and respive plots of land descd in the sd

plan on the pt of the sevl and respive grantees thrin resply named and their respive heirs exors admors and assns it was agreed that each of the sevl and respive grantees on dely to him or them of his her or their respive Conveyance and before parting with or conveying away the plot or plots thrby conveyed or any pt throf shld execute those presents

IT WAS WITNESSED that in pursuance of the sd thrinbefre recited agmt each of them the sd persons parties thrto of the 1st pt but so far only as related to the sevl and respive plot or plots of land in the sd plan inscribed with his own respive name and so far as related to the acts and deeds of himself resply and his respive heirs exors admors and assns in relation to the same sevl and respive plot or plots of land but not further did thrby for himself his heirs exors admors and assns COVENANT with the sd Wm Okell and Alexr Colquhoun Jeffrey their heirs and assns and each of them the sd Wm Okell and Alexr Colquhoun Jeffrey but so far only as related to the sevl and respive plot or plots of land in the sd plan marked with his own respive name and so far as related to the acts and deeds of himself resply and his respive heirs exors admors and assns in relation to the same sevl and respive plot or plots of land but not further DID thereby for himself his heirs exors admors and assns COVENANT with the other of them the sd Wm Okell and Alexr Colquhoun Jeffrey and his respive heirs and assns and also as a separate covnt with each of the sd persons parties thrto of the 1st pt and his respive heirs exors admors and assns in manner thrinar mentd that was to say

1st THAT not more than one dwghse shld be erected on each or any of the sd plots of land and that each such dwghse shld be of not less value than £400 exclusive of the land fences and outbldgs belonging thrto

2ndly THAT each and every such dwghse with every outbldg shld be placed 10 yards neither more nor less back from the rd including projections except those immediately adjoining the promenade wch shld be placed 8 yrds neither more nor less back including projections

3rdly THAT no stable or other outbldg shld be nearer than 10 yds from the rd boundary walls except to those houses immediately adjoining the promenade and then such stable or other outbldg shld not be nearer than 8 yds from the rd boundary walls and that the iron railings and coping fronting the rds shld be of one uniform height namely the railings 3 ft 6 in and the coping 2 ft in height the measurement to be taken from the crown of the road opposite and that the division fences to the extent of 10 yds back from the road be built or constructed of iron stone or brick and if constructed of iron shall not exceed 3 ft in height and that no temporary fence shld be made but such as shld be approved of by the sd persons parties thrto of the 1st pt

4thly THAT no mill steam engine brewery chemical works lime kiln glass work or slaughter-house shld be erected on any pt of the sd sevl plots or parcels of land

5thly THAT there shld never at any time be carried on upon any of the sd sevl plots of land or upon any pt throf resply or in any bldg erected or to be erected upon any of the sd plots of land any of the trades manufactures and businesses following that was to say soap boiler candle maker skinner or tanner brewer manufacturer of acids or alkalies retailer of malt or spirituous liquors or any other trade manufacture or business whatsoever

6thly THAT in case any bldg shld be erected or begun to be erected on any pt of any of the sd plots of land marked with the name of any of the sd persons parties thrto of the 1st pt contrary to the stipulations and agmts hereinbefre contd then and in any and every such case and when and so often as the same shld happen it shld be lawful for the sd Wm Okell and Alexr Colquhoun Jeffrey or the survivor of them his heirs or assns or other the trustees or trustee for the time being under those presents to enter into and upon any and each parcel of land whereon any such bldg shld be erected or be begun or be in the course of erection respivy and to abate and pull down every such bldg or by Bill in equity to enjoin and restrain the erection throf and that in case any bldg shld be erected or be begun to be erected on any pt of any of the sevl plots of land marked with the name of either of the sd persons parties hereto of the 2nd pt contrary to the stipulations and agmnts hereinbefore contd then and in any and every such case and when and so often as the same shld happen it shld be lawful for the other of them the sd persons parties hereto of the 2nd pt or his heirs or for any of the sd persons parties hereto of the 1st pt his heirs or assns to enter into and upon any and each such plot land whereon any such bldg shld be erected or be begun or be in the course of erection respivy and to abate and pull down every such bldg or by Bill in equity to enjoin and restrain the erection throf

7thly THAT each and every of them the sd persons parties to those presents and his respive heirs exors admors and assns shld and wld from time to time contribute and pay a due and just proportion in respect of the plot or sevl plots of land in the sd plan marked with his name respivy and of the dwghse on each such plot erected or to be erected in common with the owners of the sevl other plots of land descd on the sd plan of all costs charges and expenses wch had been already incurred and wch shld from time to time and at all times thrar be incurred in or about the forming and constructing and the maintaining and keeping in good repair and cleansing and scowring as well of the sevl roads or ways descd in the sd plan and of the sea wall promenade and lodge as also all and every the main drains and main sewers already made or thrar to be made in or upon any pt or pts of the land descd in the sd plan for the common use convenience and advantage of the owners for the time being of the sd sevl plots of land descd in the sd plan and of the dwghses erected or to be erected thron respivy or for the general and common drainage of the same lands and that the expense of lighting the sd rds or ways with gas shld be contributed and pd by theowners of such dwghses as for the time being shld be erected on the sd plots of land and as shld be completed and fit for habitation or in equal shares and proportions and that for such respive proportionate share of all such costs charges and expenses as afsd of any of the sd persons parties hereto of the 1st pt or his or their respive heirs or assns or the owner or owners for the time being of any of the sd plots of land inscribed on the sd plan with the name or names of any of the sd persons parties hereto of the 1st pt or of the dwghse or dwghses thron erected who shld refuse or neglect to pay such proportionate share of such costs charges and expenses the sd Wm Okell and Alexr Colquhoun Jeffrey or the survivor of them or his heirs exors admors or assns or any other the trustees or trustee for the time being under those presents shld when and so often as such refusal or neglect shld happen have full power to distrain upon and shld and may distrain upon the plot of land messuage or dwghse or sevl and respive plots of land messuages or dwghses the owners or respive owners whereof resply shld have made such default or refusal in the same manner as landlords are authorised to do for rent in arrear and dispose of such distress or distresses accordingly and that for such respive proportionate share of all such costs charges and expenses as afsd of either of the sd persons parties hereto of the 2nd pt or his respive heirs or assns or the owner or owners for the time being of any of the sd plots of land inscribed in the sd plan with the name or names of either of the sd persons parties hereto of the 2nd pt or of the dwghse or dwghses thereon erected who shld refuse or neglect to pay such proportionate share of such costs charges and expenses the other of them or the exors or admors of such other the trustee for the time being shall when and so often as such refusal or neglect shld happen have full power to distrain upon and shall and may distrain upon the plot of land messuage or dwghse of the or the sevl and respive plots of land messuages or dwghses the owner or repive owners throf shld have made such neglect or refusal in the same manner as landlords are authorised to do for rent in arrear and dispose of such distress or distresses accordingly

8thly THAT no sewer shld be opened or broken into without leave of the trustees for the time being and in case the owner or owners of any of the sd plots of land or any person or persons employed by him or them shld do any manner of injury or damage to the curb stones sewers or ways or roads on the sd lands by reason of bldg on any such plot or plots of land or by any other means every such owner his heirs exors admors and assns shld immediately repair and make good such damage or if he shld neglect or fail so to do for the space of 14 days after the damage or injury done then it shld be lawful for the sd trustees or trustee for the time being or any of them to cause all such repairs to be made and done as they or he may consider necessary to such curb stones sewers and ways or roads and forthwith and by any legal process to recover all expenses throf from the owner or owners causing such damage to be done

AND LASTLY THAT the sevl and respive persons parties to those presents resply and their respive heirs and assns and the respive owners for the time being of the sd sevl and respive plots of land inscribed in the sd plan with the names of the sd persons parties to those presents resply and of the respive dwghses erected or to be erected thron resply shld and wld from time to time and at all times herear abide by submit to and observe all such lawful and reasonable rules and regulations as shld from time to time be made by or on the pt of the owners for the time being of the same sevl plots of land at any meeting to be held as hereinar mentd for or in relation to the promoting of the better and more convenient and advantageous enjoyment of the whole of the same plots of land and the dwghses thereon or for or in relation to the contribution by the owner or owners for the time being of each of the sd plots of land of the means necessary towards the expenses of keeping in repair the sd roads sea wall promenade and lodge and main drains and sewers and of lighting the sd roads with gas

AND the sd Wm Okell and Alexr Colquhoun Jeffrey do hereby for themselves their heirs exors and admors covenant with each of the sd persons parties hereto of the 1st pt and with his respive heirs exors admors and assns that they the sd Wm Okell and Alexr Colquhoun Jeffrey their heirs and assns do and shall stand seized of and interested in all the roads descd in the sd plan and thron coloured yellow and of the sd promenade

UPON TRUST to permit and suffer the same at all times for ever herear to be left open and unbuilt upon and be freely used and enjoyed by the sd sevl and respive persons parties to these presents and by their sevl and respive heirs and assns and by the owners and occupiers for the time being of the sd sevl and respive plots of land nod. from 1 to 174 inclusively upon the sd plan and of the sevl and respive dwghses erected thron resply

AND IT IS HEREBY AGREED AND DECLARED between and by the sd sevl persons parties to these presents that the sd roads and promenade shld at all times for ever herear be left open and unbuilt upon and be freely used and enjoyed by the sd sevl persons parties to these presents and by their respive heirs and assns and by such occupiers as afsd

AND for the ppose of agreeing and determining upon the expenses to be from time to time incurred in keeping the sd roads promenade sea wall lodge and sewers in repair and for lighting the sd roads with gas and also for making and determining upon the rules and regulations to be observed for the better more convenient and more advantageous enjoyment of the sd sevl plots of land and the dwghses erected and to be erected thron and for securing all other objects of those presents it was thrby agreed and declared between and by the sd persons parties to those presents as follows that was to say:-

THAT there shld be one General Meeting of the proprietors for the time being of the sd plots of land and dwghses in every year to be held on the first Monday in July at the Clarendon Rooms in South John Street in Liverpool or at such other place in Liverpool or Aigburth as might from time to time be agreed upon at any Meeting or otherwise And an Extraordinary Meeting may also be held at any time when and so often as the Trustees for the time being of the sd roads or the proprietors for the time being of 20 or more of the sd plots of land shld convene the same.

THAT of every meeting general or extraordinary 7 clear days notice in writing specifying the time & place of meeting and as to every extraordinary meeting specifying also the business for wch the same is convened shld be sent by post or otherwise to the proprietors of the sd sevl plots of land.

THAT the presence of ten or more persons being proprietors of 20 or more of the sd plots of land shld be necessary to constitute any meeting and unless the requisite number attend within one hour after the time appointed and also remain until the business of the meeting be disposed of such meeting shall be dissolved

THAT every meeting shld in the first place choose a chairman from among themselves and every proprietor present in person or by proxy (such proxy being a proprietor) shld be entitled to vote as follows namely the owner of one plot one vote the owner of two and under six plots two votes the owner of six plots and under ten plots three votes the owner of ten plots and upwards four votes but if two or more persons shld happen to be owners as joint tenants or tenants in common of any one of the sd plots of land they shld only have one vote among them in respect of the same respive plot of land and all questions shld be determined by a majority of votes the chairman to have a casting vote besides his own private vote in case of an equality

THAT the determination or resolution of any such meeting shld be binding on all the sd persons parties to those presents and their respive heirs and assns but that no expenses for repairs or otherwise shld be incurred except such as shld be sanctioned by some general or extraordinary meeting unless any accident shld occur as the bursting of a sewer or any destruction by storm or otherwise of the sea wall requiring immediate repair

THAT no rule regulation or determination of any meeting shld be annulled or altered but by the determination of two successive subsequent general meetings

THAT the trustees for the time being shld cause a book to be kept in wch the proceedings of every meeting shld be entered and the entry of such proceedings of every meeting shld be signed by the Chairman throf and that any general meeting shld have power from time to time (notice throf having been given in the summons convening the meeting) to remove any person or persons from being a trustee or trustees of the sd roads sewers promenade sea wall lodge and land and to appoint another or others in his or their stead

AND IT IS hereby further agreed and declared between and by the sd persons parties to those presents that the sd William Okell and Alexr Colquhoun Jeffrey their heirs and assns shld stand seised of and interested in the sd plot or plots of the sd land wch shld not be allotted or taken by any of the sd persons parties thrto and also of the lodge

UPON TRUST to let the same for the benefit of the shareholders for the time being according to their respive shares throf but subject to the control of any meeting of the shareholders as afsd and as to the sd last mentd plot or plots of land and (if any meeting shld so direct) also as to the sd lodge UPON TRUST that they the sd trustees for the time being did and shld sell and absolutely dispose of the same resply by public auction or private contract subject to all such covnts conditions and restrictions as were thrinbfre expressed and contd concerning the other of the sd plots wch had been taken by the sd persons parties thrto for the best price or prices in money that could be reasonably obtained for the same with liberty to buy in at any auction or auctions and to rescind or vary the terms of any contract for sale and to resell by either of the modes afsd without being responsible for any loss or expense occasioned thrby and did and shld receive the moneys to arise by such sale or sales and give a receipt or receipts for the same wch receipts or receipts shld effectually exonerate the purchaser or purchasers his her or their heirs and assns from all responsibility as to the application of the money thrin expressed to have been recd and from all obligation to enquire as to the regularity or propriety of the sale or as to the regularity or propriety of the appointment of any new trustee or trustees of the prems if any such appointment shld have been made and did and shld apply the moneys to arise by such sale or sales after defraying throut all expenses incident thrto towards the expenses of making and maintaining in repair the sd roads promenade sewers sea wall and lodge and if there shld be any surplus then do and shld pay the same between and to the sd persons parties to those presents according to their respive shares throf

AND IT WAS THRBY LASTLY agreed and declared that when and so often as any vacancy shld happen in the number of the trustees of the sd roads promenade sewers sea wall lodge land and premises by the death resignation or removal of any of the trustees for the time being it shld be lawful for any meeting convened as afsd of the proprietors for the time being of the sd plots of land alotted to be taken by the sd persons parties thrto to appoint a new trustee to supply and fill up every such vacancy and thrupon the sd roads promenade sewers sea wall lodge and premises shld from time to time be conveyed so that the same may be vested in the continuing trustees and such new trustee jointly

UPON the trusts thrinbre declared and contd or such of them as shld be subsisting and capable of taking effect and every such new trustee shld have and might exercise and execute in conjunction with his co-trustees all the powers and authorities thrinbre contd or such of them as shld be subsisting or capable of taking effect

EXECUTED amongst other parties by Richard Willacy Godwin, William Carter, James Redcliffe, William Cawlett, John Bennett Thomas Walker.

Index

The index covers the text and the Appendix but not the notes, in the following lists: PERSONS AND PLACES; SELECT SUBJECTS; LEGISLATION AND OTHER PARLIAMENTARY BUSINESS; TABLE OF LEGAL CASES

PERSONS AND PLACES

For individuals mentioned only in respect of a legal case whose title names them, see the **Table of Legal Cases** below. Relevant entries are assembled under the following general heads: *The Judiciary and legal sources*; *Liverpool streets and other localities* (parks/estates excepted); *Parks and estates*.

Abram, Thomas 111, 112
Aldred, William 30
Anson, Sir William 48, 50
Astley, Mr 112, 115
Atkinson, Samuel 36
Avison, Thomas 74, 77, 139
Avison and Morton 76
Backhouse, Miss 72
Bacon, Francis 5
Bagshot 50
Baker, Peter 88
Ballantyne, Robert 105, 106
Banning, Revd Benjamin 87
Banning, Thomas 87, 89
Banning, Thomas Haines 87
Banning, William 87
Barber, Thomas 92
Bath 15
Beauclerk, Topham 87
Bedford, Duke of 11, 12, 35, 36
Bedford House 35
Bennett, John [snr and jnr] 99-101, 103-105, 112, 116, 155
Benton, Thomas 30
Bernard, Margaret 72
Berwick-on-Tweed 19
Birkett, James 74, 77, 139
Birkett, Thomas and William 77

Birmingham 2, 11, 21, 55
Bisbrown, Cuthbert 66
Blackburne family 87, 88
Bleasdale, Robert 110
Bloomsbury 11, 35
Bolton, J. 109-112
Bostock, Walter 104, 116, 118, 119
Bower, William 75, 139
Bradford 104
Brighton 15
British Museum 35, 36
Broadhurst, Henry 16
Brown, 'Capability' 6
Bunnell, William 72, 77
Bushby, William Peatt 72
Calke Abbey 12
Cameron, Charles F. 139
Carlisle 19
Carlton Palace 37
Carter, George B. 75, 77, 139
Carter, Robert Knott 90
Carter, William 155
Cawlett, William 155
Chalcots 27
Charles II 7
Cheadle 90
Cheltenham 39

Churchill, Lord Randolph 16
Collins, Henry Ward 139
Collins, Wilkie 8
Cooke, Thomas 105
Cotesworth, Charles 74, 77, 139
Covent Garden 11
Cragg, John 71, 72
Croft within Winwick 87
Crook, Mr R.S. 101, 106
Davies, John 103, 105, 108
Davison, Henry 105
Dawson, James 147
Dawson, John 88, 90
Dempsey, Mr 71
Devonshire, Duke of 19
Dodge and Wynne 114
Dolphin, Robert 55
Doran, Thomas 100-102, 105, 109,
    113
Dyer, Mr 108
Eden, John 74, 77, 139
Edgbaston 2, 11, 27
Egham 50
Emley, Frederick 51
Eton College 27
Evans, Captain 107, 108
Evans, Edward 104
Fairclough, James 108
Felixstowe 42
Forsyth, Thomas 74, 75, 77, 132-
    134, 136-139
Forwood, T.B. 75, 139
Gateshead 19
Gill, - 113
Gillespie, William [snr and jnr] 104
Godwin, Richard Willacy 155
Goore, William Henry 74, 139
Gould, - 108

Grace, Mrs 109
Grace, Thomas 107-110, 120
Gray, Mr 108, 109
Grosvenor, Lord 11
Halsall, Thomas 118, 119
Hanson, Mr 120
Harpur, Sir Henry 12, 13
Harrison, Arnold 87, 88
Harvey, Enoch 19
Hatton, Thomas 87
Hill, George 103
Holme, Samuel and James 74, 76,
    77, 139
Holmes, Henry 89
Holt, John 74
Hope, Peter 100
Hope, William [snr and jnr] 23,
    87, 88, 100, 105, 106, 109
Horsfall, Abraham 104, 119
Huddersfield 19
Huthersall, - 119
Hutton, William 105
Ingram, James 105, 106
Ireland/Irish 65, 67, 69
Ireland, Henry Gardner 90, 91,
    104, 105, 107, 114, 115
James I 11
Jeffrey, Alexander Colquhoun 100,
    104, 105, 113, 116, 117, 148-
    154
John, [king] 65
Jones, Harriet and Maria 100
Jones, Inigo 11
Jones, James Fisher 105
Jones, Mr/John 101-103, 105-7,
    113-116
Jones, Robert 102
Jones, William 73

The Judiciary and legal sources
A'Court, P.M.   58, 61
Blackstone   29
Bracton   29
Brougham, Lord   38
Cottenham, Lord Chancellor   38, 40
Cotton, Lord Justice   41
Cross J.   54
Eldon, Lord   36, 37, 40
Farwell J.   30
Gale, C.J.   29
Holdsworth, W.S.   29, 30
Jessel, Sir George   40
Jolly, W.A.   40, 50, 58
Knight-Bruce V.C.   40
Lindley, Lord   58
Megarry J.   60
Millett J.   52
Parker J.   59
Phillimore, Lord   56
Prideaux   59
Romilly, Lord   41
Scott L.J.   30
Shadwell, Sir Lancelot, V.C.   37-40
St Leonards, Lord   41
Wray, Chief Justice   30

Kenna, P.   107
Kenton   51
Kershaw, William   102, 115, 116,
    118, 119
King Edward School   21
Knowles, Ellen   92
Lace, Ambrose   77, 139
Lancaster   132
Langsdale, Mr   108
Lawson, William   14
Lee, John Yate   74, 77, 139
Leicester Square   18, 41

Leyland, John   89-92
Leyland, Ralph   100-103, 105,
    114-119, 122, 141, 145
Leyland and Earle   91
Lightbody, Robert   89
Lincoln's Inn Fields   11

Liverpool streets and other localities
(parks/estates excepted)
Liverpool   3, 5, 8, 9, 13-16, 19, 20,
    23, 39, 40, 43, 47, 49-51, 53,
    57, 61, 65-70, 72, 73, 76, 77,
    79, 87-90, 99, 102, 104, 107,
    111, 116, 120-123
Abercromby Square   14
Aigburth/Road/Vale   71-75, 87-91,
    94, 99-101, 105, 109, 110,
    120, 153
Canning Street   75
Castle Street   68
Childwall   110
Clarendon Rooms   11, 91, 105, 153
Cook Street   76
Dale Street   68
Everton   65, 69, 71, 91, 101
Exchange Buildings   72, 73
Falkner Street   102
Fullwood Lodge   72
Garston   87-89, 117, 118, 120, 121
Grace's Farm   107, 109, 110, 120
Harrington   66, 69, 70
Huskisson Street   37, 75
Island Farm/Road   89
John Street, South   101, 153
Liverpool Athenaeum   77
Liverpool Exchange   89, 99
Mary Ann Street   101
Moss Lake Fields   14
Myrtle Gardens   61

Otterspool 87, 88, 121
Paradise Street 104
Parliament Street 65
Rodney Street 65
Rose Vale 111
Seel Street 73
St Anne Street 65, 72, 75
St George's, Everton 71
St Mary's, Grassendale 100, 120
St Michael's in the Hamlet 72
South Hill 73
Walton 70
Water Street 68, 69
Wavertree 65, 69, 70
West Derby 11, 70
Western/Eastern Drive 94
White House farm 72

London 5-8, 11, 13, 15, 16, 18,
    40, 52, 118
Loudon, John Claudius 6, 7
Maitland, Fowler 27
Manchester 47, 49, 50, 67, 121
Maryport 19
Matthews, William 21, 22
Maybrick, Florence 120
McNeile, Elizabeth 77
McNeile, Revd. Dr Hugh 71, 73,
    74, 77, 139
Mercer, John 14, 15
Mersey, River 87, 88, 99, 133-136
Milburn, Jane 92
Miller, Joseph 75, 139
Milner, E. 8
Molyneux, Charles William 65
    [and see Sefton]
Montagu, Ralph 35
Montagu House 35
Morton, Hugh 51

Moss, Mr 14, 88
Myers, - 77, 104
Myers, William, jnr 139
Nash, John 7
Newcastle 19, 51, 121
Nickson, Joseph 111
Norfolk, Duke of 20
Nottingham 2, 121
Ockleston, Robert 90
Ockleston, William 89-91, 104,
    105
Okell, William 100, 104, 105, 113,
    115, 116, 148-152,
Okill, Charles 14, 15
Parker, Charles Stewart 74, 75, 77,
    132-134, 136-139

Parks and estates
*Park/s (general) 2, 3, 5-9, 15, 19,
    23, 47-49, 51, 53, 61, 62,
    65-79, 87-94, 99-105, 107,
    109-112, 118-122, 127*
Axwell Park Estate 51, 52
Birkenhead Park 8
Calthorpe Estate 11, 21, 28
*Cressington Park Estate 3, 23, 53,
    78, 79, 87, 89, 94, 99-104,
    107, 120-122, 148...155*
Crystal Palace Park 8
Darras Hall Estate 51, 52
Derby Estate 19, 65
Dock Estate 13, 68
Four Oaks Estate 54
*Fulwood Park Estate 65, 71-79, 87,
    91, 93, 102, 120, 132...140*
*Grassendale Park Estate 78, 87-89,
    91, 92, 94, 99-104, 107, 109,
    111, 112, 120-122, 141...147*
Green Park 7

Hyde Park 7
Princes Park 8, 71, 105
Regent's Park 7, 8
Salisbury Estate 19
Sandfield Park 49, 121
Selly Hall Estate 56
Selly Hill Estate 56
St James's Park 7
Stocksfield Estate 51, 52
Tadworth Park Estate 62
Toxteth Park 65-73, 87, 111, 132
Victoria Park/Company/Trust 47-49, 121
Wentworth Estate 50
Woodend Park 94

Paxton, Joseph 8, 71
Pearce, John 90
Preston 72
Pritt, A.D. 14
Radley, James 90
Ramsgate 38
Redcliffe, James 155
Repton, Humphrey 6
Rickman, Thomas 71, 72
Rigge, Thomas 77, 139
Roche, James 104
Rodick, James Dawson 90, 92, 141
Roscoe, Edward Henry 77, 139
Routledge, James 108
Rowan, James 89-92, 105, 107, 141, 146
Royal Victoria Hotel 39
Rowson, Mr 107
Russell, Lord 35
Sandbach, T., and Co 75
Savoy Hospital 87
Seddon, Joseph 90
Sefton 19, 65, 66, 70-72

Shand, - 104
Sheffield 19-21, 47, 122
Simpson, George 20
Smith, Alexander 72, 73
Smith, Alexander, jnr 132-140
Smith, Mary 72
Smith, William 72, 73, 77, 132-140
Smith, William Digby 73
Smith, William Warren 105, 113, 115
Southampton House 35
Southport 57
Stanleys 65 [and see Derby]
Stewart, John 70
Strand, (the river) 87-89, 93. 144
Summers, George 105, 107, 108, 111, 113-115
Summers, Henry 113, 114
Sutton Coldfield 54
Sweet, George 40
Tarleton family 87, 88
Tarrant, W.G., Ltd 50
Tayleur, Mr 71
Tomlinson, William John 74, 139
Turner, Charles 90
Tyrer, John 105
Ulverston 108
Vaughan, Lady Rachel 35
Vaughan, William 104
Wakinshaw, Joseph Whiteside 51, 52
Wakinshaw, Revd William 52
Walker, Thomas 155
Warrington 87
Watts, Joseph Angelus Dominic 100-102, 104, 109, 115
Webster, John 66
Whalley Abbey 87

White, Dalrymple 57
William I 1
Willis, William Valiant 89-92, 141,
    146
Wilson, Eliza 104
Wilson, Joseph 104
Wolf, John Starr de 89-92, 141,
    146
Woodhouse, W. 72

Woods, Commissioner of 37
Woods, George 115
Woolwright, John 87-92
Workington 19
Wynne, Robert 74, 114, 139
Yates, Richard Vaughan 71
Young, Mr 107, 108, 110, 111
Younghusband, J.P. 75

SELECT SUBJECTS

Agreement, legal 37, 39, 77, 89-92
Agreement, Articles of 72-74
Aigburth Land Company,
    First/Second 141, 148
Amenity/ies 3, 5, 7, 8, 12, 14, 17,
    22, 30, 47, 49, 60, 62, 69,
    78, 79, 122, 127-129
Appeal, Court of 54
Appropriation of landscape 6, 7, 77
Barratt [Development plc] 61
Building/s 2, 6-9, 11-14, 16-18,
    21-23, 27, 28, 30, 33, 36-39,
    41-43, 47, 48, 50-52, 54-62,
    65-68, 70, 75, 76, 78, 92-94,
    102, 107-109, 112, 121, 122,
    127-129, 142, 150-152
Building land 6, 22
Building leases 8, 9, 11, 13, 27, 66
Building schemes 2, 33, 37-39, 42,
    47, 50, 51, 54-56, 58,
    127-129
Building society/ies 17, 42
Chancery, Court of 13, 18, 32, 35,
    57, 60, 61, 119
Committee of management 3, 49,
    50, 52-54, 61, 75, 91, 92, 99,
    101-103, 105-117, 119-122

Conservation 17, 43, 58, 79, 94,
    121, 128
Conveyance 43, 48, 50, 56, 59, 73,
    88-90, 92, 93, 100, 101, 103,
    106, 107, 111, 114, 128
Corporation, Liverpool 13, 15, 19,
    50, 66, 70, 121
Corporation, Manchester 50
Council, Town, Liverpool 13, 14,
    61, 68, 70
Courts 30 [and see Appeal,
    Chancery, Equity, High
    Court]
Covenant/s 5, 8, 9, 14, 17, 18,
    20-23, 27, 32-43, 36-43,
    47-62, 74-76, 78, 79, 91-94,
    102-104, 114, 117, 119-122,
    127, 128, 132, 134, 141, 148,
    149
Covenants, amenity 22
Covenants, mutual 38, 39, 43,
    50-54, 59, 102, 122, 127
Covenants, negative 33, 42
Covenants, positive 17, 18, 23, 24,
    33, 37, 41, 53, 60, 79, 92,
    121, 128

Covenants, restrictive 5, 9, 18,
   20-24, 27, 28, 33, 37, 42, 51,
   53, 56-58, 60, 72, 92, 94,
   121, 127, 128
Conservative Land Society 41
Daily Telegraph 61
Deeds 2, 43, 49, 51, 54, 59, 92,
   93, 102, 106, 107, 116
Easements 28-30, 53, 128
Ecclesiastical Commissioners 19
Equity, Court of 34-42, 90, 139,
   142
Family settlement 27
Freehold 1, 2, 5, 8, 11, 12, 16-22,
   32, 33, 37, 39, 41, 47, 57,
   59, 60, 62, 65, 67, 70, 72,
   76, 122, 123, 127-129
Garden/s 5-7, 36, 37, 39, 41, 62,
   75, 76, 91, 93, 115, 121
Garston Land Company 88
Grass fund 117, 118
Injunction 34, 36-41, 51, 54, 58
Land 1, 2, 5, 6, 8, 11-15, 17-22,
   27-37, 39-42, 47-49, 51, 53,
   56, 57, 59-62, 66-68, 70-74,
   87-92, 99-101, 103-109, 114,
   115, 122, 132-139, 141-144,
   148-154
Landlord 1, 2, 11, 12, 14, 16-18,
   22, 27, 32, 61, 70, 122, 123,
   127, 128
Landowner/owning 1, 6, 11, 12,
   17-20, 27, 28, 30, 31, 38, 39,
   47, 70, 122
Landscape 6-8
Lands Tribunal 50, 58, 59, 120
Law 1-3, 5, 9, 17, 19, 21, 23,
   28-36, 38, 40-42, 49-53, 56,
   69, 77, 79, 102, 128, 129

Law Commission 51
Leasehold/leasing 1, 2, 5, 8, 9, 11,
   14-22, 27, 32, 57, 59, 60, 70,
   121, 128
Leasehold defects 21
Leasehold enfranchisement 16, 18,
   22
Leasehold Enfranchisement 16
Leasehold Enfranchisement Society
   18
Leasehold reform 22
Liverpool Gaslight Company 69,
   111
Liverpool Land Company 88
Liverpool Mercury 16, 99, 105
London and North Western Railway
   Company 118
Management 3, 9, 12, 50, 55, 61,
   91, 115, 119, 123, 129 [and
   see Committee of ...]
Manorial jurisdiction/rights 69, 87,
   88, 118
Mersey Iron Foundry 71
Nuisance 28-32, 52
Parkinson, Sir Lindsay, and
   Company Ltd 50
Parliament/parliamentary 12, 13,
   15, 16, 34, 47, 48, 50, 65-68,
   71, 118, 129
Planning (concept) 5, 8, 17, 27,
   58, 71, 92, 128
Prescription 28-30
Privy Council 11
Promenade/esplanade 51, 53, 92,
   93, 100, 111, 112, 117, 121,
   148-150, 152-154
Real property 32 [and see Royal
   Committee ... real property]
River rights 28

Road/s, (obligations re) 33, 36, 39,
   53, 55, 78, 117, 121, 133,
   136, 137, 141, 146, 148, 150,
   151
Sea wall 53, 92, 93, 100, 101,
   107, 108, 142, 145-148, 150,
   152-154
Settlement/s 12, 16, 35, 92,
   99-103, 106, 112
Sewer/s 49, 51, 69, 74, 75, 92, 93,
   110, 111, 116, 133, 136, 137,
   142, 144-147, 150-153

Termes de Ley, Les 28, 29
Tithe 72, 74, 120
Tontine 48, 71
Town and Country Planning 22
Trespass 29
United Services Club 37
Wall 65, 76, 90, 108, 112, 115-
   117, 135, 141, 146, 149 [and
   see Sea wall]
Wirral Freeholders Benefit Society
   16

LEGISLATION AND OTHER PARLIAMENTARY BUSINESS

Toxteth Park Estate Act 1775   70
Prescription Act 1832   29
Parliamentary Boundaries Commission, report 1832   67, 73, 89
Royal Commission on 'Law ... real property', reports 1832
   32-35, 37-38, 40, 41, 48
Municipal Corporations Act 1835   13, 15, 68-70
Victoria Park Act 1837   48
Transfer of Property Act 1844   51
Settled Land Act 1882   13
Leaseholders' Enfranchisement bills 1883-5   15
Royal Commission on the Housing of the Working Class 1884   18
Select Committee on Town Holdings, report 1889   18, 22, 70
Land Registration Act 1900   2
Acquisition of Lands (Asssessment of Compensation) Act 1919   57
Law of Property Act 1925   50, 56, 79
Wentworth Estate Act 1954   50
Leasehold Reform Act 1967   17, 27, 128
Civic Amenities Act 1967   17
Leasehold Reform Housing and Urban Development Act 1993   17, 128

TABLE OF CASES

Aldred's Case 9 Co.Rep 57   30
Baxter v. Four Oaks Properties Ltd [1965] Ch.816   54
Bristow v. Wood (1844) 1 Coll. 480   40
Chandler v. Thompson (1811) 3 Camp 80   31
Dolphin's Conveyance, Re. (Birmingham Corporation v. Boden and others)
    [1970] 1 Ch. 654   55
Duke of Bedford v. Trustees of the British Museum (1822) 2 My & K 552   35
Earl of Zetland v. Hislop 7 App Cas 427   59
Elliston v. Reacher [1908] 2 Ch. 374; affd.[1908] 2 Ch. 655
                                 42, 43, 47, 54-56, 59
Foss v. Harbottle (1843) 2 Hare 461   49
Four Oaks Properties Ltd. v. Hadley and others CA (*The Times*) 2.7.1986
                                   54, 121
Halsall v. Brizell [1957] Ch. 169   23, 32, 43, 53-55, 121
Henman's Application, Re. P & CR 1970 102.   50
Higgins v. Betts [1905] 2 Ch. 210   31
Keppell v. Bailey (1834) 2 My & K 517   38
Knight v. Simmonds [1896] 1 Ch. 653; affd [1896] 2 Ch.294   58
McVittie v. Bolton Corporation [1945] KB 281   31
Mann v. Stephens (1846) 15 Sim 377   40
Price and another v. Bouch and others [1986] 53 P & CR 257   51, 52
Rankin v. Huskisson (1830) 4 Sim 13   37
Roper v. Williams (1822) Turn & R 18   36
Schreiber v. Creed (1839) 10 Sim 35   39
Spencer's Case (1583) 5 Co.Rep 166   21
Tulk v. Moxhay (1848) 2 Ph 774   18, 40, 41, 42
Whatman v. Gibson (1838) 9 Sim 196   38